THE
WONDER
YEARS

THE WONDER YEARS

40 WOMEN OVER 40
On Aging, Faith, Beauty, and Strength

LESLIE LEYLAND FIELDS, *editor*

Kregel
Publications

CONTENTS

Always

INTRODUCTION

I am looking into the mirror. Not the "mirror, mirror on the wall," which kindly tells me whatever I want by a quick dim and flick of the light switch, but the far scarier one: the mirror in my hand that magnifies my face by a factor of ten. Under this painful scrutiny, I skip over my pores and crow's-feet and go right for the brows. I count a record number of grays. With jaw set I pluck them ruthlessly, realizing I'll soon be brow-less at this rate. What then? I have no idea. Thankfully, the mirror is minute enough to keep me from cataloging all the other marks of age upon my body. Today, it's just the brows.

Tomorrow it might be something else, especially if I have given in to my secret online obsession with celebrity slideshows. Particularly the "Where Are They Now?" slides, documenting actors' unforgiveable lapses into middle and old age. How dare our movie icons age like that? The disgust is palpable. Those galleries are usually linked to celebrities trying to escape the ignominy of aging, who end up instead in the next slideshow: "The Worst Plastic Surgeries Ever."

Who wants to age, really? We fight it in so many ways, some of which are downright silly. Recently I saw an enticing online headline that had gone viral: "The Hairstyle That Will Get a 38-Year-Old Carded."

I clicked on it, of course. There she was: a woman obviously in her late thirties, peering goofily from behind long, blunt bangs once popular among tweens and teens. At least they weren't pigtails! But this obsession is hardly new. Remember Twiggy, the seventeen-year-old supermodel-waif from the sixties, who suddenly made mature women everywhere long to look eleven years old?

Are we so youth-obsessed that we long to be children again? Perhaps. Who wouldn't love another chance at childhood, to do it right and thorough with the proper joy next time? But maybe all this is more than the universal human hunt for the fountain of youth and innocence. Maybe it's something more modest, more possible. Maybe we older women just want to be seen again.

In 2013, *Salon* ran a provocative article by Tira Harpaz with the headline "Women over 50 Are Invisible." The essay made significant waves among women over fifty but was, predictably, ignored by others. The author's thesis was simply this: "If you want to make a person invisible, just put her in the shoes of an over-fifty woman and abracadabra, watch her disappear."[1] Harpaz, herself in her late fifties, described aging and its accompanying invisibility as a kind of fading away into irrelevance, including "a loss of attractiveness and sex appeal, the end of fertility, a glimpse of a slow, lingering decline."

I will not entirely deny this. And, I am told, even women just over forty begin to feel it. One Sunday after church, I was talking to a friend about this book, which began as *The Happy over Fifty Women's Guide to the Best Half of Our Lives*. She said, "Oh no. I need this book. I'm forty-three and I'm feeling it already. Invisible. Not young anymore. People look right through me now." I stared at her, not looking through her, but remembering myself at that age. She was right. When I hit forty, I noticed it as well, though I assumed I was erased from the roster of "those who matter" because I often had a river of children streaming behind me. Motherhood does indeed usher us out of the rooms of power and status, but age accomplishes this far more effectively. So this book opened further, wider.

You will not hear a litany of laments here, however, nor even many complaints. Not even from Win Couchman in her essay, "The Grace to Be Diminished," where she describes finally giving up her car keys and her independence. Most of us are too busy for complaints. The day I plucked my gray brows, I climbed a mountain here in Kodiak. I started up the trail slowly, admiring the spruce trees arrowed to the sun, the peregrine falcons and bald eagles kiting the vast sky over the ocean. I reached the summit an hour later, panting but legs muscled and strong. Just a few miles to the east, close enough for me to touch, it felt, stood the Three Sisters, three steep, trenched peaks. I see them often, but standing there that day, I saw them anew, admiring their stolid immovability.

How many raging Alaska storms had they survived? I knew it was those very storms, and time itself, that had adorned those slopes with their majestic patterns of erosion.

I'm not crazy about erosion on my own face, but I thought about women ahead of me, women I admire who are two and three decades older than I: Doris with her glowing red hair and killer figure. Luci with two new books coming out this year; Vera who still teaches dance classes; Kay, still speaking around the world. I thought of Iris Apfel draped in turquoise or orange with layers of massive jewelry lighting her tiny figure. When she attended Paris Fashion Week, she was treated like a combination of a rock star and Queen Elizabeth. She is drop-dead gorgeous. And she is ninety-four. And not least among them, Merle with her servant's heart and generosity to all.

All of these women are well past eighty. I am agog not at their age; there are plenty of nonagenarians and even centenarians knocking around. But a ninety-four-year-old setting new fashion trends? A ninety-ish woman who is still making new friends? An eighty-eight-year-old still creating stunning poetry? An eighty-three-year-old opening fresh biblical truths to hungry audiences? Beauty and age have too long been enemies and antitheses. But times are changing. And so are we. Dozens of models over sixty grace fashion runways and magazine covers, flaunting their wrinkles, wearing their gray hair long and flowing as they pose elegantly among women young enough to be their granddaughters. Even in this dizzying technological age, which prizes the nimblest brains and the quickest adapters, we women over forty are proving again and again that innovation and imagination can flower all the way into our nineties.

Even more than this, as I look around my faith community, I see older women serving. I see them beginning new ministries after their retirement, finding new ways to alleviate suffering and lighten others' loads. Here are the real radicals, women who reject the prevailing notion of our culture that age delivers a license for freedom and self-indulgence. How many times have I heard celebrities and acquaintances alike, on the eve of their fiftieth or sixtieth birthday, proclaim to the world, "Watch out. It's my time now. I'm gonna say and do whatever I want." And in the next breath, when asked for their newfound wisdom, they invariably say something like, "I've finally come to love myself just as I am. Now I don't have to please anyone but myself." Is that really all there is? Did we survive childhood, adolescence, and our twenties and thirties to arrive on the doorstep we left as children? Surely not.

I'm not saying aging is a breeze. Vanities and losses remain, I confess. This book is something of a coming out for me. I've vacillated over the last few decades about making my age public. Sometimes I deliberately hide my age or even lie. A few months ago, I changed my date of birth on Facebook to a full decade younger, thinking, *Why not? Why should I reveal that I'm almost a senior citizen?* I speak to university audiences often and would rather *not* be perceived as their mother or, worse, their grandmother. But it didn't stand long before I was spasmed by guilt and tried to change it back, only to find the date uneditable. (It seems you can only change your age twice before the FB police come after you.)

Like many others, sometimes I am mistaken for someone ten or even fifteen years younger, given good lighting and the just-right dress. But other times it cuts the other way, which feels like the ultimate defeat. But why?

Why do we feel as though we're racing against time? And as if time were not an inequitable enough racing partner, some of us, mostly subconsciously, lace up our shoes next to photoshopped magazine cover models who regularly go under the needle and the laser, who work out four hours a day with their personal trainer, nibbling salads devised by their personal chefs. For a few, their own postmenopausal youthfulness has become their single raison d'être.

It's a rigged, impossible race. Mostly, we know it. Our best claim, then, is to look or feel younger than our actual age. Here, finally, we're crowned a winner in the lifestyle sweepstakes, which is not so much about cheating death—we're not concerned with that . . . yet. But to cheat time itself, and even more, to cheat nature, which, by the time we're over forty, we know for sure is not our mother.

How then do we respond to the passing years that make their inevitable marks upon our faces, our bodies, and our abilities? A thousand different ways. For me, my life is still expanding. I turn sixty this year and never have I felt so alive. As I write this, I'm working on two books, packing for a research trip to Europe, and getting ready to fly to fish camp, where I'll work in commercial fishing all summer (but I won't work in the boats much, conceding to the limits of my body). This is not to say, "Look at me," but rather, look at you. Look around. Look and listen to these forty women, most of whom are just like you and me, women who are growing, beginning new ventures, casting off old shadows, whose own passages through life and time have yielded great fruit, even when aging saps health, energy, and abilities. Yes, even then. Welcome to the party!

But we're serious, too. Aging is not for the thin-boned or the faint of heart. As we climb year by year, whether it's a mountain or a ladder, we need to stop for a long moment and consider the view. We need to ask questions. Maybe we should even check our ladder. As a number of writers have told us, we could spend our entire lives climbing the ladder of achievement and success only to discover, once we mount those upper rungs, that we've leaned the ladder against the wrong wall. It takes courage to stop and take stock of who we are, where we've been, and where we're going. It takes strength to keep our hearts open. It takes fearlessness to keep questing after the good, the beautiful, the true. We'll do exactly that in these pages, knowing that no matter our age, it's never too late to keep becoming the women God wants us to be.

These are indeed the Wonder Years. In writing and compiling this book, I have been astonished and inspired by my fellow writers. I know you will be as well, but we have another audience in mind too. We're taking up the mantle the apostle Paul gave us in Titus 2:3–5, for "older women" to "teach what is good" to "younger women." All of us in these middle and later years have gained a storehouse of memories and experiences that surprise us in their depth and breadth. We find ourselves, unexpectedly at times, experts in a whole host of areas: We're mothers and grandmothers, wives, mothers-in-law, and stepmothers. We're professionals. We're farmers and fisherwomen. We're pastors, writers, teachers, ministry leaders. As we have learned, stumbled, and grown, we must pass on all that is good and true to those coming behind us. Many of us had no such encouraging voices as we lurched through our own earlier years. We send these notes on to you, our younger sisters, with joy and love. We commit ourselves to easing your passage as well!

How shall we do this, then? Our lives seldom divide into neat packages, but the three sections of this book make enormous sense to all of us in our "years of wonder." Along with the passage of time comes courage, a wise sort of adventuring that knows how fleet is the passage of time and how ripe the moment for new experiences, so we begin with "Firsts." The wisdom that launches us into new ventures also relieves us of burdens and obligations we no longer need to carry. The next section is "Lasts," where fourteen women cast off the weight of regret, fear, judgments, and perfectionism. Finally, though we're constantly changing and growing through the embrace of the new and the loss of the old, we arrive as well at our "Always" convictions. We discover again the core of who we are and who we vow to remain, no matter our health, our abilities, or our age.

Welcome to the Wonder Years! Get ready for breakout joy, indulgent abundance, heart-stopping wisdom, and never-let-go faith!

Notes

1. Tira Harpaz, "Women over 50 Are Invisible," Salon.com, April 5, 2013, https://www.salon.com/2013/04/05/wanna_know_what_its_like_to _disappear_try_being_a_woman_over_50_partner/.

Firsts

It is never too late to be what you might have been.
GEORGE ELIOT

What is possible for us in our forties, fifties, sixties, seventies, and beyond? Sometimes we need reminding. Consider the oldest woman in this section, **Luci Shaw**, who embarks on her first wilderness canoeing trip in her early seventies, paddling all day in the waters off British Columbia, often in heavy rain, and camping at night on rocky shores. The youngest here, **Lauren Winner**, embarks on a decidedly inward adventure, paving the way for risks and journeys of another sort entirely. **Charity Singleton Craig** gets married for the first time at age forty-two, changing the way she thinks about her body. **Amy R. Buckley** and her mother, surviving a divorce and a death, find themselves dating again at the same time, to hilarious (and sobering) effect. When her great-aunt becomes ill, **Laura Lynn Brown** pulls up stakes and moves to a new city to take care of her. **Sheila Wise Rowe** packs up her family and moves to South Africa to start a challenging ministry.

Then there are stories of the new creatures that enter our lives: **Elisa Morgan**, a dog-fearer, suddenly adopts two enormous dogs and finds her life enlarged by double. **Heather MacLaren Johnson** buys a horse farm at age forty-four and by fifty becomes an accomplished equestrian. When struck with dystonia, nearly immobilizing her, **Michelle Novak** gains a new kind of sight—and a yard full of astonishing creatures she had never seen before.

Our new capacities often surprise us, and God himself surprises us often. **Jill Kandel** writes for twenty years, following what she thought was the call of God, without publishing until age fifty-nine, when everything changes. **Jennifer Dukes Lee** finds assurance in God's cupped hands and simultaneously learns how to wean a calf. Best-selling writer **Brené Brown** repents of her dismissal of feminine handcrafts and "creativity" and joins her first art class.

A few of us have done something with our newly sagging bodies. **Amy K. Sorrells** chooses to embrace health and joy. For me, upon turning fifty, I bought my first padded bra (leopard spotted, of course).

In this kickoff section, there's no one single party line. You'll find convincing support to slow down, to speed up, to launch out into new places, ministries, relationships, and ideas. Prepare to be inspired!

Jennifer Dukes Lee

Jennifer is the author of *The Happiness Dare* and *Love Idol*. She is a storyteller and a grace dweller, blogging about faith at jenniferdukeslee.com. She is also on the writing team for DaySpring's (in)courage. A journalist at heart, she used to cover crime, politics, and natural disasters as a news reporter for several Midwestern metropolitan daily newspapers. Now she uses her reporting skills to chase after the biggest story ever: the redemptive story of Christ. She and her husband raise crops, pigs, a herd of cats, and two humans on the Lee family farm in Iowa.

Cupped Hands

You don't think your way into a new kind of living.
You live your way into a new kind of thinking.
HENRI J. M. NOUWEN

I rest my chin on our farm gate and puff out a breath of frustration. Two Angus calves with saucerlike eyes stare back at Lydia and me. On this June morning, we are chin-deep in a showdown at dawn.

These cows simply won't budge, refusing to drink from their buckets. The water's skin flutters when a lone fly drops in for a landing.

Lydia and I cajole the calves with mothering voices. Lydia chirps a rhyming tune:

> *Sherbet and Daisy,*
> *Don't be la-zyyyy!*
> *Come drink from your pail of waaaa-ter!*

But those two unyielding black calves with wet noses simply blink long eyelashes at us. I scuff at the dirt with the toe of my boot.

What they say about horses is also true for cows: You can lead them to water, but you can't make them drink.

Lydia wears worry in a knot above her brow. Her shoulders tense up with an unspoken question: *Will these calves ever learn to drink from a bucket?* Lydia kneels down, swirling the water into figure eights with her index finger. I lean beside her, rubbing reassurance into her back with tiny circles.

"It's okay, hon. We'll try again tomorrow, all right?"

Our chore pail, hidden from the calves behind the hay bales, holds two supersized bottles—the kind you'd buy if you were raising a baby Goliath or a newborn Bigfoot. Until the calves learn to drink water and eat starter feed from buckets, they will nurse from these bottles. We had hoped they wouldn't be needed today, but the calves are winning this battle of wills.

Lydia's resignation tumbles out of her mouth with a heaving sigh. She relents and marches for the hidden bottles. With her jaw clenched, she grabs a bottle of milk replacer to feed Sherbet; I take one for Daisy. We hold the bottles through an opening in the farm gate, bracing ourselves as the calves lunge at us, full tilt. These baby brutes are ravenous, like Augustus Gloop lurching toward Willy Wonka's chocolate river.

The county fair is eight weeks away. By then, the calves must be weaned. One of these graceless, 120-pound beasts will, theoretically, learn to walk behind her 55-pound surrogate mother, Miss Lydia Lee. Using a rope halter—a kind of leash for bovines—Lydia will lead Sherbet or Daisy around the 4-H show ring on a late July afternoon.

Or so we hope.

It all looks a little daunting at this point. Through the farm gate, these calves tug at their bottles with slobbering mouths. Within minutes, they drain the bottles dry and beg for more with pleading, blinking eyes.

I look down at Lydia and reassure her, "They'll learn. They'll wean eventually."

I speak with the calm confidence of someone who knows what she's doing. But it's slippery confidence and—*snap*—just like that, it's gone.

An old familiar ache rises up as I hear a sneering reproach in my head.

It goes like this: *Woman, admit it: Here's yet another farm chore that's beyond you.*

It's just a small thought—inconsequential, really. But it's right here, in these maddeningly mundane moments, that old insecurities like to make unannounced visits.

My husband—the real farmer on this farm—is helping me learn to be gentle with myself. He encourages me to try new things, like bottle-feeding calves with our daughters, even though I sometimes feel like a clumsy and inadequate farmwife.

He simply laughs and shakes his head when I retell the story of how I got myself and Daisy tangled up with the rope halter. The rope is supposed to fit over the calf's head. But I somehow slipped it on backward, and it wound itself around the calf's neck. Meanwhile, the other end of the rope circled both of my knees and one of Daisy's legs. We eventually got ourselves untangled, and while I can safely say that no animals were harmed in the making of this paragraph, my pride might have been a bit bruised. Yet Scott's good-natured response to my foible reminds me how God looks at us—"in process" and lovable, despite our mistakes.

Without regularly reminding myself of God's unquenchable love, I might be inclined to let my lousy insecurities tangle themselves like rope halters around my heart every time I make a mistake. My daughters might do the same.

Old idols are stubborn, showing up in innocent places like calf pens—exactly as they did in my grade school classrooms, corporate cubicles, and department store dressing rooms during swimsuit season. I do realize that at times the Love Idol—that desire to be loved and approved by the world—still slithers up beside me to hiss its lies into my ears, especially when I'm lacking confidence in my performance. This recognition is a victory in its own right. But still, I wish the Love Idol were permanently silenced.

Two calves' tails twitch. Wide, begging eyes plead, *More.*

Both bottles have been sucked dry. Defeated, Lydia and I walk up the hill to wash before breakfast. Just as these calves will one day be weaned, God is weaning me.

In the mudroom, I turn on the faucet and wash bottles. Milky water swirls down the drain.

It feels like a sort of inner cleansing, an act of faith, to stand here at the sink, watching dirty water drain away. It's an inner turning, a refocusing, a flipping over.

I have to remind myself daily what I already know: Focus on the Father, not on the flaws. Look to the Savior, not the self. The Messiah, not the mirror. This is the power of the gospel: Water cleanses, through the Word.

I feel victorious in Jesus, having made the conscious choice to drink from Living Water instead of the bottled praise of humankind. Yes, "like a weaned child is my soul within me" (Psalm 131:2 NLT).

A patient Father can lead his child to water, but he doesn't make her drink it. He holds water out, as if in cupped hands. He bids her, *Come and drink.*

And at the edge of this sink, where all the grime has drained away, I drink again from those hands. I sing back to the Father, and I look full in the Savior's wonderful face, soaking in the beauty. I repeat memorized Scripture about who I am, about how I've been fashioned by God, created to do good works that will bring his kingdom glory, here below. There is no earthly yardstick, rating system, ticker, or scale to measure that sort of worth.

The water runs clean, and I can feel it now—how when I've shifted my focus, anxiety drains away. This is what I have been learning and relearning: Look upward, not inward.

It's real. And it's really changing everything.

The Lord didn't ask for us to prove our significance to the world. Or to prove ourselves to him. He didn't ask us to prove anything at all. *He* is the one who approves, declaring us beloved. Christ asks again for our whole hearts and our willingness to drink living water from his cupped hands.

Just then, it dawns on me. *My hands.* I turn off the faucet and call for Lydia. "Come quick, honey! I've got an idea. I think I know how to wean Sherbet and Daisy."

She pulls on her boots again, and I tell her what we'll try. She's giddy with hope, giggling a stream of joy all the way back down the hill. The gravel crunches under our boots. A barn swallow swoops overhead. The morning breeze whistles in our ears.

The gate creaks open with an easy push, and we call out for the calves. "Sherbet, Daisy!" They peek out the barn door with those blinking saucer eyes.

"Will it work, Mom?" Lydia asks. "Will it work this time?"

I bend down on my knees beside a five-gallon bucket. Two calves step closer, curious and tentative.

I dip both my hands into the tepid water. If they won't come to the water, then I can bring the water to them. I lift my cupped hands, filled with water, like a chalice. I inch forward on my knees, with those hands held out as an invitation, and then I slip water under the wet nose of one still-thirsty calf.

And right then—from cupped hands stretched out on an early morning, in this common place where God's glory slides like gold across the water's surface—it happens. A baby learns to drink.

Brené Brown

Brené is a research professor at the University of Houston Graduate College of Social Work. She is the author of three No. 1 *New York Times* best sellers: *The Gifts of Imperfection, Daring Greatly,* and *Rising Strong.* Her most recent book is *Braving the Wilderness: The Quest for True Belonging and the Courage to Stand Alone.* Her TED talk "The Power of Vulnerability" has over thirty million views. She lives in Houston, Texas, with her husband, Steve, and their children, Ellen and Charlie.

Cultivating Creativity

Some of my best childhood memories involve creativity, and almost all of them are from the years that we lived in New Orleans, in a funky, pink stucco duplex a couple of blocks from Tulane University. I remember my mom and me spending hours painting wooden key chains shaped like turtles and snails, and making crafts out of sequins and felt with my friends.

I can vividly see my mom and her friends in their bell-bottoms coming home from the market in the French Quarter and making stuffed mirlitons and other delicious dishes. I was so fascinated with helping her in the kitchen that one Sunday afternoon she and my dad let me cook alone. They said I could make anything I wanted with any ingredient that I wanted. I made oatmeal-raisin cookies. With crawfish boil spices instead of cinnamon. The entire house stank for days.

My mom also loved to sew. She made matching shift dresses that she and I wore (along with my doll, who also had her own tiny matching dress). It's so strange to me that all of these memories that involve creating are so real and textured to me—I can almost feel them and smell them. They also hold so much tender meaning.

Sadly, my memories of creating end around age eight or nine. In fact, I don't have a single creativity memory after about fifth grade. That was the same time that we moved from our tiny house in the Garden District to a big house in a sprawling Houston suburb. Everything seemed to change. In New Orleans, every wall in our house was covered with art done by my mom or a relative or us kids, and homemade curtains hung over every window. The art and curtains may have been out of necessity, but I remember it being beautiful.

In Houston, I remember walking into some of my new neighbors' houses and thinking that their living rooms looked like the lobby of a fancy hotel—I vividly remember thinking at the time, *like a Howard Johnson or a Holiday Inn.* There were long heavy drapes, big sofas with matching chairs, and shiny glass tables. There were plastic plants with hanging vines strategically sitting on top of armoires and dried flowers in baskets decorating the tops of tables. Strangely, everyone's lobby kinda looked the same.

While the houses were all the same and fancy, the school was a different story. In New Orleans, I went to a Catholic school and everyone looked the same, prayed the same, and for the most part, acted the same. In Houston I started public school, which meant no more uniforms. In this new school, cute clothes counted. And not homemade cute clothes, but clothes from "the mall."

In New Orleans, my dad worked during the day and was a law student at Loyola at night. There was always an informal and fun feel to our lives there. Once we got to Houston, he dressed up every morning and commuted to an oil and gas corporation along with every other father in our neighborhood. Things changed, and in many ways that move felt like a fundamental shift for our family. My parents were launched on the accomplishments-and-acquisitions track, and creativity gave way to that stifling combination of fitting in and being better than, also known as comparison.

Comparison is all about conformity and competition. At first it seems like conforming and competing are mutually exclusive, but they're not. When we compare, we want to see who or what is best out of a specific collection of "alike things." We may compare things like how we parent with parents who have totally different values or traditions than ours, but the comparisons that get us really riled up are the ones we make with the folks living next door, or on our child's soccer team, or at our school. We don't compare our houses to the mansions across town; we compare our yard to the yards on our block. When we compare, we want to be the best or have the best of our group.

The comparison mandate becomes this crushing paradox of "fit in and stand out!" It's not cultivate self-acceptance, belonging, and authenticity; it's be just like everyone else, but better.

It's easy to see how difficult it is to make time for the important things such as creativity, gratitude, joy, and authenticity when we're spending enormous amounts of energy conforming and competing. Now I understand why my dear friend Laura Williams always says, "Comparison is the thief of happiness." I can't tell you how many times I'm feeling so good about myself and my life and my family, and then in a split second it's gone because I consciously or unconsciously start comparing myself to other people.

As far as my own story, the older I got, the less value I put on creativity and the less time I spent creating. When people asked me about crafting or art or creating, I relied on the standard, "I'm not the creative type." On the inside I was really thinking, *Who has time for painting and scrapbooking and photography when the real work of achieving and accomplishing needs to be done?*

By the time I was forty and working on this research, my lack of interest in creativity had turned into disdain. I'm not sure if I would categorize my feelings about creativity as negative stereotypes, shame triggers, or some combination of the two, but it came to the point where I thought of creating for the sake of creating as self-indulgent at best and flaky at worst.

Of course I know, professionally, that the more entrenched and reactive we are about an issue, the more we need to investigate our responses. As I look back with new eyes, I think tapping into how much I missed that part of my life would have been too confusing or painful.

I never thought I'd come across something fierce enough to shake me loose from my entrenched beliefs about creativity. Then this research came along . . .

Let me sum up what I've learned about creativity from the world of Wholehearted living and loving:

1. "I'm not very creative" doesn't work. There's no such thing as creative people and noncreative people. There are only people who use their creativity and people who don't. Unused creativity doesn't just disappear. It lives within us until it's expressed, neglected to death, or suffocated by resentment and fear.
2. The only unique contribution that we will ever make in this world will be born of our creativity.
3. If we want to make meaning, we need to make art. Cook, write, draw, doodle, paint, scrapbook, take pictures, collage, knit, rebuild an engine, sculpt, dance, decorate, act, sing—it doesn't matter. As long as we're creating, we're cultivating meaning.

Literally one month after I worked through the data on creativity, I signed up for a gourd-painting class. I'm not even kidding. I went with my mom and Ellen, and it was one of the best days of my life.

For the first time in decades, I started creating. And I haven't stopped. I even took up photography. It might sound cliché, but the world doesn't even look the same to me anymore. I see beauty and potential everywhere—in my front yard, at a junk store, in an old magazine—everywhere.

It's been a very emotional transition for me and for my family. Both of my kids love art, and we do family projects together all the time. Steve and I are Mac addicts, and we love to make movies together. Last month, Ellen told us that she wants to be either a chef or a "life artist" like my friend Ali Edwards, who inspires both of us. At this point, Charlie loves to paint and would like to own a booger store (which is both creative and entrepreneurial).

I also realized that much of what I do in my work is creative work. Writer William Plomer described creativity as "the power to connect the seemingly unconnected." My work is all about making connections, so part of my transformation was owning and celebrating my existing creativity.

Letting go of comparison is not a to-do list item. For most of us, it's something that requires constant awareness. It's so easy to take our eyes off our path to check out what others are doing and if they're ahead or behind us. Creativity, which is the expression of our originality, helps us stay mindful that what we bring to the world is completely original and cannot be compared.

Michelle Novak

Michelle lives in Delevan, New York, with her two huge dogs, Sundew and Acacia. When able, she roams the hills, swamps, fields, and forests of western New York State, often bringing back specimens to examine under a microscope. She is a lifelong self-taught linguist who studies seventeen languages and is able to translate four, including Greek and Hebrew. Her current study project (in addition to insects and birds) is a five-year-long immersion in Leviticus, where she is working out a creation and temple theology that culminates in Christ.

Of Bodies and Birds

I knelt in the swamp, mesmerized by the creature on the shrub. His strange contortions enthralled me: he was emerging from his exuvia—breaking out of his outer shell, undergoing the change from water-based nymph to fully-adult dragonfly.

I watched for more than an hour. It looked excruciating, bone cracking, the outer layer splitting along what we might call the spine. Finally, he emerged—at first a faint greenish color not so different from the spent gray insect he was. When I bent the twig down for a better look, he wobbled onto my hand. There, to my delight, he finished coloring to a deeper emerald, drying and straightening his wings. When he was finally erect, the process nearly finished, he rubbed his head on my palm to loosen his antennae, whirred his brand-new wings for a few seconds, and flew away. I decided to keep the twig where the cracked and empty shell was still attached. I understood entirely how this felt: it mirrored my own bone-cracking transformation to wholeness.

I had always been athletic and energetic. I had even been a lifeboat crewman in the Coast Guard, as well as a shipboard navigator who climbed onto buoys in bays and the ocean, using my sextant to fix their position. Even as I approached fifty, I still led a vigorous life and was untroubled at the thought of aging.

Until one day. Without warning, my neck swelled up, became hot to the touch, and my head fell over. My neck could not support my head. Afraid to move, I slept that way in a chair only to wake up the next morning with my head rammed hard onto the opposite shoulder, along with a spine-cracking sensation and pain I couldn't begin to describe.

My head never went back. As I waited months to see a specialist, I thought of obtaining illegal and heavy drugs, or suicide. Mostly, I crawled on the floor, letting my head drop onto it over and over, sobbing and groaning, hoping I would die.

I was eventually diagnosed with systemic dystonia, a complex neuro-muscular disorder for which there is no cure and very little in the way of successful treatment. The dystonia affects almost every muscle in my body, with constant tormenting spasms in my neck muscles and sur-prise spasms everywhere else, twisting my spine, wringing it from top to bottom. It rapidly progressed, bringing with it a deep fatigue and a violent tremor in my hands and neck. I had no idea how much I'd be able to do, but I knew my active life was over.

What was possible for me in this new life, this new-old body? If this was how I was going to age, I at least wanted peace of mind in the midst of it. That meant I needed something to study. I've always been active both in body and in mind. I love studying languages and have gained proficiency in several living and dead languages, which I use to translate ancient texts, particularly the Old and New Testaments. I knew if I was going to survive this dystonia, I needed a new mental challenge, but I could only study for short periods. I also desperately needed something to keep me moving. Even the little movement I could tolerate was crucial to keeping as healthy as I could be.

One winter morning, as I rummaged through my books, I happened upon my mom's old bird guide. The cover was gone, and it had seen much use. I smiled as I fingered through it, remembering how she loved to tell me the names of all the birds in her yard: the tanagers, the purple martins, and especially the hummingbirds. She had several feeders set up exclusively for them, and would sit and enjoy their antics for hours. The memory of how bright and happy she became when she talked about the hummingbirds remained.

Then I remembered something else: by then, she too had developed a spastic rigidity in all her limbs and lost most of her ability to move about safely. But she was so rejuvenated when watching or talking about the birds.

I made a decision. I got a couple of feeders and put out some seeds. Soon the birds came—first the usual, chickadees and titmice. And then woodpeckers, which fascinated me. By spring I had an outdoor aviary only an obsessive-compulsive, twisted central nervous system could dream up! The yard was full of new birdsong and vigorous life.

Most of my outdoor time now was spent slowly working through each feeder, moving, filling, and cleaning it. I experimented. I started talking to the birds, and they began to come closer, forgiving the twisted body and maybe even the twisted mind of one who talks to birds.

I learned to listen to the incredible arias of bird language, as they discuss, announce, and proclaim their intentions for their every movement and activity.

Many nights I study about them. And since my disorder requires me to sit for hours at a time every day, I've learned to observe them in their own space through a disciplined, almost athletic stillness, a great accomplishment for someone whose muscles are still yanking, twitching, and spasming.

Now, every day a world of creatures alight in my flawed garden to be tended by a wracked body. I know what I look like. I move like someone twenty years older. But the creatures come. They stay. I'm charmed and I feel deep affection for what I never noticed when I could see straight ahead.

When my head was permanently wrenched to the right by the unyielding spasming of many neck muscles, my eyes were recast. What was peripheral vision has become my central vision. Only a twisted body can know it and navigate the world by it.

The direction of my life has been realigned as well. I move sideways. I move slowly, with what might be seen as excruciating deliberation to those who only see straight ahead. But the best part is, I see small. I see slow. What I used to blow by in fast hikes, I now stop to examine, write about, photograph, and consider. That's how I met my dragonfly.

And my chickadee. At the end of May, as I was filling a chickadee feeder, talking as I worked as was my custom, a chickadee landed on a branch just a few inches from me. He looked at me, his head as cocked to the side as the dystonia had tilted mine. I slowly raised my hand, asking in a soft voice, "Would you like a seed?"

In a moment, he flitted into my palm. I liked the soft pinch of his feet and he seemed to like sinking into the flesh of my hand. We looked at each other with the same long quizzical gaze. A few seconds later, he lit from my hand to the tree. We were companions now. I knew he would stand in my palm again. He came because I held my hand out to the birds from January to almost June. In my old life, I would never have had the patience to wait and be still.

As it is with everyone whose soul is hidden in Christ, my brokenness has been redeemed, and I am whole. I'm twisted but whole. I know who I am: I am a helpless creature who must wait on the Lord for every good thing.

And he has cared for me in my new state and allowed me to care for others. I have a pair of robins nesting in my yard that come when I call them. I named them as Adam must have when things were new and slow, and he had fresh eyes allowing him to truly see every wonderful creature that God presented to him, creatures that came to him as these come to me.

They wait for the food I give them. They drink and bathe in the water I pour out for them. They frolic and nest in the trees and grass I tend for them. I've finally learned why the birds made my mother so joyous, even in her pain and immobility.

And in these creatures, I see a new world coming when my body is made as whole as my soul. In that day, I will crawl out of my broken exuvia and stand erect to feed my chickadees with strong, steady hands.

Jill Kandel

Jill grew up in North Dakota, riding her Appaloosa bareback across the prairie. She married a man from the Netherlands and worked overseas for ten years in Zambia, Indonesia, England, and the Netherlands. Kandel's first book, *So Many Africas: Six Years in a Zambian Village*, won the Autumn House Nonfiction Prize and the Sarton Women's Literary Award. Kandel is working on a second memoir, set in the Netherlands. She blogs about writing life and living between cultures at her website, jillkandel.com.

Turning

The first time I heard God's whisper, I was five years old, sitting under an apple tree in my back yard. My mom handed me a napkin inked with red words.

"See if you can memorize this poem," she said. I nibbled my sandwich and turned to the words.

> Thank you for the world so sweet,
> Thank you for the food we eat,
> Thank you for the birds that sing,
> Thank you, God, for everything.
> (Edith Rutter-Leatham)

These words arrived in a way I'd never felt before: alive. I attached myself to them, or they to me. The beginnings of a lifelong yearning for words and for God.

The first time I set foot on the continent of Africa, I was a twenty-six-year-old North Dakota prairie girl, a bride of six weeks married to a man from the Netherlands. He'd signed a contract with the Dutch government on our honeymoon. Johan would be teaching agriculture to subsistence farmers in rural Zambia.

After arriving in the capital city, we boarded a Zambian bus and proceeded west. Twenty hours and six flat tires later, we came to the provincial capital, Mongu. We walked to the harbor and boarded a banana boat canoe sporting a thirty-five-horsepower engine. We puttered up a languid river covered in white water lilies. Brightly plumed birds flew alongside. We entered various tributaries and crossed over the mighty Zambezi River where massive hippos twitched their tiny pink ears at us and roared. We joined the Luanginga River, continuing west. Ten hours later, sunburnt and sore, we turned a corner in the river and stopped on a dark sand beach. Kalabo Village. My home for the next six years.

~

Kalabo Village holds so many firsts and so many memories. How could it not? Our first house: a concrete, two-bedroom rambler with a flurry of bats living between the wilting ceiling boards and the tin roof. Cockroaches infested the kitchen. The occasional snake hid behind the toilet.

Our first daughter was born in Kalabo Village, one month early, weighing six pounds. She was a suction delivery and we thanked God the electricity worked. I have a picture of myself from that day. I am wearing a loose plaid shift and lying on a delivery room table that's crooked with age and rust. My dark brunette hair is sweaty and tied back in a long ponytail. A dirty pillow lies under my head, stamped in red letters: Government Republic of Zambia. After her birth, I stayed one hour, then went home. Happy for a fan that worked.

A year later, we had a son.

It was in Kalabo Village that I first learned the sound of God's silence. I couldn't even sense his presence through all the sorrow: starvation, malnutrition, disease, civil war. A car accident, a child dead. His silence roared as I shattered.

When I left Africa, she did not leave me. I carried her with me in my blood: bilharzia, giardia, hepatitis, and dysentery along for the ride. It took two years before the doctors figured them all out.

After a decade abroad living in Zambia, Indonesia, England, and the Netherlands, we arrived back in North Dakota, my husband pursuing his PhD in agriculture, my heart a hole of bitterness. I was forty and pregnant with our fourth child. Sad. Confused. Silent. My hair already mousy-gray. I cut it shoulder length. Disgusted at being pregnant and gray, I began to dye it brown.

Cheer up, Buttercup. Hadn't I always been the good girl? The chin-up, God-has-a-wonderful-plan-for-your-life girl? I felt betrayed by God, by my husband, and by my life. I pushed Africa out of mind and moved on, living as if I'd never even heard of Zambia.

A gap. A hole. A scream.

The only remnant, my daily nightmares, waking up in the dark, my body sweaty, my hands shooing invisible flies away.

After Johan's graduation, we moved to a town of less than one thousand people. I became an invisible stay-at-home mom. I couldn't even see myself. But God could.

One night, standing under a starlit sky, I thought I heard God's whisper. I'd known his voice for what seemed like my entire life. The whisper of it in the Word. The solid truth of it from the pulpit. The rationality of it taught at Bible school. And still it startled me. It had been so long. I'd almost forgotten the sound of it.

I cocked my ear and turned toward heaven.

I thought I heard him calling me to write.

"Write?" I asked quizzically. "I don't have an English degree; I'm forty-two years old."

It wasn't really a conversation so much as an orientation, a tilting toward, a turning to. I wish I could explain. God is hard to explain. His voice even more so. As I strained to listen, I remembered Bible stories and discussions between God and man.

Abraham said he was too old and laughed at God. Jeremiah said he was too young and he didn't know how to speak. God didn't seem to be overly concerned about their qualifications or their ages.

∼

The nudge of God's voice grew in me and I watched with curiosity as circumstances conspired. My librarian invited me to join a writing club. I did. They asked for a story about Africa. I wrote about a snake. My husband said he'd watch the kids when a writing workshop opened up not far from us. I went. I wrote about our daughter's birth in Kalabo Village and it made my instructor cry.

I began getting up early, writing from five till nine before the four kids got up and life took over. I met other women writers online and we formed a critique group, reading each other's work. I studied the art and craft of writing as if my life depended upon it.

And I wrote.

It was the writing that began to peel back the layers, open the wounds, and allow God to heal.

∼

I wrote for sixteen years.

I wrote my way through a house move, a job change, Lyme disease, my kids' high school graduations. I wrote through my forties and into my fifties. I wrote my way out of pain and anger and sorrow.

And then a funny thing happened. I remembered the blue-tongued lizard. I remembered the yellow weaver birds. I remembered the small chirping geckos with their padded adhesive toes, clambering up the walls while my children laughed and pointed.

"Gecko! Gecko!" they shrieked.

I remembered the joy.

I sent my stories out and accumulated rejection slips, over one hundred of them at one point, but I also got acceptances. Essay followed essay. And then I joined the stories together into a book. It was far from done. Three rewrites later, adding arcs and metaphors and an older voice looking back—*why did I go, who was that young woman, did we accomplish anything*—and my book was finished. I sat at the keyboard with nothing else to say.

That night, my nightmares stopped. I'd written them away.

I spent the next year studying agents, publishers, contests, and shopping my manuscript around. I was a fifty-eight-year-old writer with a decent résumé and no degree, thinking I could break into the publishing world. Nobody seemed to care.

I wondered if I'd really heard God's voice.

My children moved out and found their own lives. My oldest son married. I became a grandmother. The night after my grandson was born, I came home at midnight from visiting and had an email waiting.

"Call me. I have some information that might interest you," the email said. It came from Michael Simms at Autumn House Press. I'd sent my manuscript in to them about nine months earlier. What could they want?

The next morning, still dazzled by the birth of my first grandbaby, still feeling the gentle weight of him in my arms, I called Michael Simms. The cell phone shook in my hands.

"We want to publish your manuscript," he said. "It won first place."

I had to ask him to repeat himself.

"There were about a thousand entries," he continued. "We chose yours in the memoir category."

I was fifty-nine years old. A publisher wanted my book. I had dreamed so long about this moment, worked for it, believed in it without believing.

A grandmother. A book.

I shook my head and smiled until I cried.

This is the gift of aging: it gives a different perspective. He has turned my mourning into dancing. I am in my sixties now. I've been dyeing my hair for over twenty years. Most of those years, I've been brunette, the color of my childhood, the color of comfort. For the past six years, I've been a redhead, a playful color, the color of joy.

I recently said to Johan, "I think I'll quit dyeing. It's pure white, you know."

He turned to me and smiled.

He said, "I like it red."

Laura Lynn Brown

Laura is a writer, editor, coach, teacher, and speaker whose work has been noted in *Best American Essays*. A native Ohioan, she lives in Pittsburgh, Pennsylvania, by way of Arkansas. Her first book, *Everything That Makes You Mom: A Bouquet of Memories*, guides readers in mining memory to write tiny vignettes that add up to a portrait of their mothers. She has taught online writing workshops for Tweetspeak Poetry. Her recent writing obsessions include friendship, food, play, walking, tea, and elder care.

Where Have All the Hearing Aids Gone?

My great-aunt was in the hospital. An emergency room nurse inventoried her belongings. Shoes, slacks, blouse, sweater, one watch, two rings, one hearing aid. . . Wait. She wears two. Maybe it had come off when the blouse was pulled over her head?

The nurse had helped my aunt undress and insisted there had been no hearing aid in the right ear. My aunt was stable and resting, waiting for a doctor who was busy at another hospital.

"I think I'll go look in your apartment for that hearing aid," I said loudly in her good ear.

She encouraged me to go. "You don't need to stay with me. Don't let me keep you from what you have to do."

The first time I had searched for my aunt's lost hearing aid, I'd flown from Arkansas to Pittsburgh and was visiting her in an independent living facility. We were getting ready for bed, and she knew as soon as she pulled her top over her head that it had dislodged a hearing aid. She grew increasingly fretful as we looked in the bedclothes, under the bed, in the trash can, and everywhere else in the radius of where it might have traveled. Nothing.

I had heard stories from family members about searching for lost hearing aids and the distressing cost of replacing them. While both touching and funny when listening to the story from far away, it was a different story when it was me trying to find the tiny putty-colored gadget, the same hue as her carpet.

It had to be somewhere. What were we missing? I tried the last place I could think of. And there it was—inside the toe of her slip-on sneakers.

Four years had passed between that first search and this one, which was probably my fifth or sixth. On the week of that first search, I had flown up to spend time with my father, who had just started treatment for lung cancer. It took eight months from his diagnosis to his death, and in my frequent trips back to the Ohio-West Virginia-Pennsylvania tristate area, my heart tilted more and more steeply toward home. My brother and stepmother and I grew closer through the bonds of stress and grief. I glimpsed what I had missed by living in the South for most of my adult life.

The second time I looked for my aunt's hearing aid was a year ago during another hospitalization in a rehab hospital. She was in the midst of a common cycle for elderly women: an infection, a fall at home, a hospital stay to get the infection under control, a few weeks of rehab to regain strength and balance before going home. Family converged; I flew up from Arkansas, and others came from West Virginia, Ohio, and Texas. How many family members does it take to find a missing hearing aid? Many to search, one to spot: under the bed.

During that visit, I thought, *It's time*. It's time for someone to live in the same city as she did. There were loving family members living an hour away from her and there were reasons for her to stay put in Pittsburgh, including long relationships with her doctors and the cognitive decline that accompanies any major change for most elderly people.

Six weeks from the day I decided and said, "I'm moving," I took occupancy of my new Pittsburgh apartment.

In caregiving, there are all kinds of firsts. The first time you drive someone to a doctor's appointment. The first time you search for the missing TV remote and find it in the storage compartment of a Rollator walker. The first time you help with toileting. The first time you take your loved one to her favorite restaurant and have to gently stop her from making her third lap around the salad bar because she didn't remember that she'd already been there.

There's the first time you discover some of her cash is missing. The first time you take her to church and incur her displeasure because she thought you were taking her to *her* church, but it hasn't existed for fifteen years. The first time you get a call from her facility that she's been taken to the hospital. The first time you are stunned and stung by a "You are not the boss of me" lecture.

There are other kinds of firsts, too. The first time I took her to my new apartment and she marveled at the clouds. The first time I took her to the grocery store—though she always mildly complains about the fifty-yard walk from her studio apartment to the elevator—and she happily walked five times that distance around the store, attracted by the fresh vegetables and intrigued by a pyramid of cheese crackers.

"We choose without knowing what we're choosing," Wendell Berry writes in one of his poems. I knew moving back to my home territory after twenty-five years away would be choosing to be closer to most of my family, and it would involve both joys and frustrations. I knew that choosing to leave a twenty-year newspaper career for the uncertainties of self-employment as a writer and editor would be a difficult leap, one I might not have had the courage to make if I wasn't making other leaps at the same time. I knew that it would be choosing adventure. What I can't know for sure, but I don't doubt, is how this might have been chosen for me, directed by the God who helped me to find an apartment a five-minute walk from a vibrant church and who daily gives me opportunities to choose to live for something, someone other than myself.

What I didn't know is how much I would be choosing to advocate for her, a job that requires skills I am sometimes developing on the fly. When hospital employees see the tiny, white-haired, hard-of-hearing ninety-four-year-old in front of them, they sometimes address me as if she can't hear. And they patronizingly ask, "How far did she go in school? . . . So was she a housewife, then?"

"She never married," I say. "She started at the phone company as an operator and worked her way up as a vice president supervising hundreds of people. She's always been very independent." And suddenly they glimpse the vibrant life that came before and see the spark in her eyes and hear the complex-compound structure of her sentences on her best days.

There will be other firsts, I know. Possibly the first time she doesn't know who I am, or worse, who she is. For now, there are all these things that give meaning and direction and challenge to my life. And there is someone—one of the few remaining now that both of my parents are gone—who has known and loved me all my life.

"Thank you for everything you've done," she says whenever we part. I can't even remember the first time she said it. Sometimes she adds, "Especially for the things I don't remember or don't even know about."

On that last hospital stay, when I went to her home and looked for her hearing aid, I found it under her bed, behind a suitcase. How on earth did it get there?

When I got back to the hospital, I handed her the hearing aid, and she tried to fit it into her right ear, but she couldn't make it stay. Wait a minute . . .

I asked to see the one in her left ear, then held them up side by side. Identical.

This must be the one that was lost the last time her left hearing aid was replaced. "Well, always good to have a backup," I quipped.

And we did what she does daily—what I hope we will do for many years to come—we laughed.

It may be a cliché, but it's true for hearing aids, and lost coins, and family ties, and things I have yet to discover with her. What once was lost has now been found.

Lauren Winner

Lauren writes and lectures widely on Christian practice, the history of Christianity in America, and Jewish-Christian relations. Her books include *Girl Meets God, Mudhouse Sabbath, A Cheerful and Comfortable Faith, Still: Notes on a Mid-Faith Crisis,* and *Wearing God.* She has written for *The New York Times Book Review, The Washington Post Book World, Publishers Weekly,* and *Christianity Today.* Dr. Winner, an Episcopal priest, is vicar of St. Paul's Episcopal Church in Louisburg, North Carolina.

Forty

The rabbis teach that you're not to study *kabbalah*—mysticism—until you reach forty. As Maimonides puts it, "It is not proper to dally in *pardes*"—the orchard of mysticism—"till one has first filled oneself with bread and meat; by which I mean knowledge of what is permitted and what forbidden, and similar distinctions in other classes of precepts."[1] In other words, learn the basics of Torah and law before you begin to ponder the ten vessels that originally contained God's light but couldn't hold the glow and shattered.

The knowledge that the study of *kabbalah* was off-limits till forty set my expectations. Not that in middle age I would necessarily begin studying the Zohar, but that I might enter some wonderful orchard and discover capacities for wisdom that had been forming while I'd been busy with the essentials. Eight months ago, I turned forty.

~

The week of my birthday, I told everyone who would listen that I only knew one thing about the next decade: I knew I wanted to live my forties with some kind of intention (which, it seems to me, I didn't do in my thirties or my twenties). At various birthday lunches and cocktails, my mantra was "I don't want to be sitting here when I turn fifty, telling you that the last ten years evaporated into the fog of doing the next logical thing."

Unfortunately, I don't know how to do this—live with intention, avoid the unthinking next thing. Eight months after those conversations (which is to say one-fifteenth of the way through the decade), I'm living, it seems to me, with no more intention than I had last year, or at age twelve. Perhaps the forties are the decade of learning intention, and the fifties, should I be given them, the decade to implement the learning?

About being forty I feel by turns grateful, expectant, and remorseful. The remorse is not about having turned forty, per se. Rather, it's a gaze that looks backward to the last twenty years and finds I've wasted them. Then the gaze looks forward to the next twenty years and sees that they, too, will be wasted, cannot be otherwise, because the pattern is set: *it's as if the coming years are already wasted.* Proleptic waste.

I'm not sure what to do with this gaze. I think I should welcome her in and offer her tea. I understand she can't be seeing the whole truth, nor can what she sees be wholly true. But surely there is some truth in her prospect.

Because of what we do with our mothers' lifeshapes—and because my mother died at sixty—I assume I've no more than twenty years left, and only eighteen of them healthy. Her oncologist assures me this is not the case, that what my uterus will do has nothing to do with what hers did, but I make the assumption nonetheless.

On July 26, 1922, Virginia Woolf wrote in her diary, "There's no doubt in my mind that I have found out how to begin (at forty) to say something in my own voice; and that interests me so that I feel I can go ahead without praise."[2] At the time, she was writing *Jacob's Room*, which is, ostensibly, the story of a man's life, narrated by a woman. It's considered Woolf's first modernist novel.

~

One of the students in the workshop I'm leading is about to turn fifty, and she is worried that she's too old to do this—too old to embark on a book, too old to reacquaint herself with her youthful love of writing. I suggest she read *Writing a Woman's Life,* and I list many women who did their best work, and often began wholly new enterprises, exactly in their fifties, once their children had left home.

I find this lifeshape beautiful. It pleases me to think that a woman raising children and organizing a family and a household is also storing up knowledge and questions, and then, at age forty-seven or fifty-two or fifty-six, there is *time,* and in the time, she can turn to a different kind of work. She can bloom a new and different flower, midway through her life.

While talking to my student, I notice, not for the first time, the deep pleasure I feel about being childless. And not for the first time, I notice what the absence of children means for my lifeshape: if I have a turn in the road at fifty, it won't be because I suddenly have more time and an empty house.

~

That women—mothers—often have a new beginning after forty does not, I suspect, spare women the archetypal midlife encounter with mortality, named by Elliott Jaques in his 1965 essay "Death and the Mid-Life Crisis." Jaques hypothesized that "the central and crucial feature of the mid-life phase" is the awareness of death. "Death . . . instead of being a general conception, or an event experienced in terms of the loss of someone else, becomes a personal matter, one's own death, one's own real and actual mortality." Once death has climbed down from the shelf, we begin to see our "future as circumscribed." We see that much will, of necessity, remain "unfinished and unrealized."[3]

Jaques is right—the nearness of death isn't wholly new. My mother's death, fourteen years ago, bequeathed me a sense of mortality, and for a while, I lived as though I knew life wasn't endless. But then the gift faded; I forgot. Now the nearness of death is about me, not her.

Those are the kinds of things I thought about on my birthday, while eating Swiss fondue and chocolate whiskey cake with friends. Because much will remain "unfinished and unrealized," I'd like to live this decade with intention, by which I mean with both attention and choosiness. By which I mean I'd like to get freer of my compulsions and my careening anxieties.

⁓

Jaques, who was forty-eight when he published "Death and the Mid-Life Crisis," goes on to develop an account of the difference between the kind of creative production one does early in life and the kind of creative production one does in and after midlife. The twenty-year-old's creativity, he says, is "precipitate," done without forethought. College students can write sonatas and lyrical poetry because chords and verse are "amenable to rapid creative production." But one can't approach "sculpting in stone or painting in oils" precipitously. "With oil paint and stone," writes Jaques, "the working relationship to the materials themselves is of importance, and demands that the creative process should go through the stage of initial externalization and working-over of the externalized product. . . . The change in mode of work, then, between early and mature adulthood, is a change from precipitate to sculpted creativity."[4]

This is not to say there's no music after forty. Fanny Mendelssohn was thought by many observers to be more talented than her brother. When Fanny was born, her mother declared she had "Bach-fugue fingers," and family friends shared the opinion of the librettist and actor Edouard Devrient, who found Felix's playing "astonishing in technical execution and musical assurance, but . . . not yet equal to that of his older sister Fanny."[5]

Fanny wrote her first song at age fourteen, for her father's birthday. Twenty-six years later, she started making her compositions public, as she explained in a letter to Felix:

> Actually I wouldn't expect you to read this rubbish now, busy as you are, if I didn't have to tell you something. But since I know from the start that you won't like it, it's a bit awkward to get under way. So laugh at me or not, as you wish: I'm afraid of my brothers at age forty, as I was of Father at age fourteen—or, more aptly expressed, desirous of pleasing you and everyone I've loved throughout my life. And when I now know in advance that it won't be the case, I thus feel RATHER uncomfortable. In a word, I'm beginning to publish.[6]

Here's one small bid I've made for intention. I've been under contract for this or that book since age twenty-three. At thirty-eight, a familiar feeling knocked at my door: the impulse to write a book proposal or three. I knew I'd complete my last contracted book in about two years, just before turning forty-one, and it was time to get a new book under contract, so that the contracts would be layered over one another, so there'd be no gap—so there'd be no time to think about what I want to write, or if I want to write, or whether I want to try to write a sonnet crown instead of yet another book about Christian spirituality.

The small bid was to ignore the impulse to propose a next book to an editor. This was hard to do at first, and then it got easier, and now I've almost arrived at the blank space I aimed to create—the space where a book contract usually is.

This is a small gesture, very particular to my very particularly lucky life. I wonder how it will feel to ask myself what I want to write, and if I want to write, instead of just writing the next obvious thing.

In Jewish teaching, the number forty can betoken something new—a fetus takes forty days to form in the womb, Rav Hisda says. But the old must be cleared out to make space for the new, and forty is also about the clearing. Rabbi Zeira, who'd mastered much of the Babylonian edition of the Talmud, decided he wanted to study the Jerusalem edition. Before opening a page, Zeira fasted for forty days, so that he could forget all he'd learned of the Babylonian Talmud and make room for the Jerusalem Talmud. Perhaps Zeira was numerically imitating the flood, which required forty days to rid the world of a generation turned evil in heart.

～

I think Jaques means his account of early-life and midlife art to be taken literally. I think he means that sculptors and painters are likely to do their best work after forty, because only after forty will they slow down long enough to work with stone and paint as they require. But there's also metaphor here—that what comes now is sculpted, not hasty, and that the years of midlife are more like oil paint and marble than like rhyme. That's what I mean when I say I want intention: I want to sculpt. I want to be sculpted.

Notes

1. Maimonides, quoted in David Hartman, *Maimonides: Torah and Philosophic Quest*, exp. ed. (New York: Jewish Publication Society, 2009), 51.
2. Virginia Woolf, *A Writer's Diary*, ed. Leonard Woolf (New York: Harcourt, Brace and Company, 1954), 46.
3. Elliott Jaques, "Death and the Mid-Life Crisis," *International Journal of Psycho-Analysis* 46, no. 4 (1965): 506–7.
4. Jaques, "Death and the Mid-Life Crisis," 503–4.
5. Lea Mendelssohn and Edouard Devrient, quoted in Sarah Rothenberg, "'Thus Far, but No Farther': Fanny Mendelssohn-Hensel's Unfinished Journey," *The Musical Quarterly* 77, no. 4 (1993): 690–91.
6. Fanny Mendelssohn, quoted in Rothenberg, "'Thus Far, but No Farther'": 701.

Luci Shaw

Luci was born in London, England, in 1928 and has lived in Australia and Canada. She's the author of more than thirty-five books of poetry and nonfiction, and has lectured and taught writing workshops nationally and internationally. She received the tenth annual Denise Levertov Award for Creative Writing from Seattle Pacific University and *Image*. A lover of sailing, tent-camping, gardening, and photography, she lives in Bellingham, Washington, with her husband, John Hoyte. For further information, visit lucishaw.com.

Rowing into the Wild

I come from a family of fearless adventurers. My father was a medical missionary and explorer in the early twentieth century, the first westerner to cross the island of Guadalcanal on his own, at a time when cannibalism was common. My brother, also a doctor, has spent many months training specialists in Kabul, Afghanistan, during times of war and violence. My son, with a degree in tropical medicine, has practiced his art in South Africa among the Xhosa people and has trained medics in one of the northern ethnic regions in Myanmar while establishing a jungle school of medicine in an area rife with battle and ground mines.

My own life has felt a bit tame, wife and mother of five, with an increasing tribe of descendants. Though I have bungee-jumped in New Zealand (getting a senior discount!) and sailed the Great Lakes with a woman friend, my most risky activity has been to follow my calling as a poet in a culture where poetry is largely ignored, especially among conservative Christians. I'm not a fearful person, but the older I get (now eighty-nine) I want to maintain the balance between foolish risk and boring safety. I dread growing stale, losing energy. I know my senses need awakening.

So at seventy-one, I joined twelve others in an expedition around the South Gulf Islands of British Columbia. It was a summer course entitled

"Wilderness, Creation, and Technology" through Regent College. I wanted to test my resolve and claim my genetic identity, proving to myself that I could keep up and forge ahead even in my eighth decade.

That August I found myself on the pebbled shore of Hunterston Farm on Galiano Island. It was supposed to be the driest month of the year, yet there we were—twelve of us in full foul-weather gear, gathered in heavy rain. The Nina, our eighteen-foot craft for the coming week, was carefully packed with food supplies, cooking utensils, tents, sleeping bags, personal duffels, and a first aid kit, every cubic inch planned and designated by our leader, my good friend Loren Wilkinson. We were about to launch into the ocean to experience, observe, record, and discuss the glory of the wild in the context of current technology. Loren, a professor of interdisciplinary studies at Regent, was our gallant leader— poet, philosopher, conservationist, and lover of God and all of creation. But I confess, I was apprehensive.

Our voyage involved oars, oarlocks, and our own backs and arms. It was a *rowing* expedition. No sails, no motor, just our bodies. We would be rowing among British Columbia's South Gulf Islands, a wild, intricately beautiful part of the world, with its network of islands and channels between Vancouver Island and the British Columbia mainland. Our craft was a graceful, curving leaf of a rowboat with two masts and rudimentary sails, a replica of the boat once used by Dionisio Galiano, an explorer of this area in 1792. The Nina would carry us—or perhaps we would carry The Nina—for about 120 nautical miles.

The technology equipment for the project was minimal, but we wanted to follow as authentically as possible in Galiano's watery track. The course was for credit, with assigned readings that included Jeremy Begbie's Voicing Creation's Praise and our Bibles. Every night we were to set up camp on a different island, gather around a campfire, and discuss the day's sightings and splendors.

Standing in the rain that August day, I knew this was a serious undertaking that would involve spirit, mind, and body. I was the matriarch in this bunch of athletic younger mariners, and although I had good muscles left over from my athletic youth and summers of canoe-camping in Ontario, I didn't want to slow the others down or be a drag on my fellow adventurers. My love of the wild and the green was a carryover from my teenage days and had become the source of my writing life and a profound spiritual stimulus as well. And increasingly, as I got older, I felt the need to challenge myself. I longed to increase in both wisdom and knowledge and keep up with whatever strenuous activity I could join, hoping that age had not diminished me—yet. My spirit was vigorous. Would my bodily energy match it?

My other motivation was to find a fresh angle on the world. As a writer-photographer I know the need for a clean "lens," for a view unobstructed by old habit and the everyday. I've done a lot of tent-camping and allowed the silence of unspoiled wilderness to penetrate and refresh my busy spirit. Would this new venture allow me a virgin view of creation?

Over the next week, it stormed every day. Oilskins and Gore-Tex were never enough to keep the icy moisture at bay. Strong winds pressed the damp through every layer down to our skin and into our pores. Sleeping bags and clothes got soaked through and soggy. This should have had a chilling effect, but our effort and enthusiasm warmed us, running high, ignited by our strong motivation and expectation. By contrast, on the couple of days when the August sun shone hot, there was no shade, and there were over-friendly flies. It served no purpose to complain about either cold or heat; rather, we were buoyed by our sense of intrepidity, grateful for the one attempt at comfort—scraps of sheepskin that eased our bottoms on the wooden thwarts.

Every evening we landed on a different island—Saturna, Mayne, Salt Spring, Wallace—to camp, climbing the seaweedy rocks up to level ground on a bluff, passing the duffels up, hand to hand, setting up a flotilla of tents and a big blue tarpaulin to shield our cooking and eating and dish-washing. Loren and his wife, the dauntless Mary Ruth, were fabulous chefs, teaching us the rudiments of campfire cuisine. At night, we slept soundly in our little two-person tents (the snorers had their own!) and woke next sunrise to the smell of coffee. The cups warmed our stiff hands as we gathered to prepare breakfast before packing up and reloading *The Nina* for the new day's row ahead.

Every morning we checked the charts so that we could anticipate the tides that rise and fall up to fifteen feet in that part of the world.

Twice a day the icy sea water sweeps in and out, sucking through the narrow channels between the islands, creating savage turbulence and fierce tidal rips. Sometimes the levels of swirling waters rose level with, or even higher than, our gunwales, surging around us as we struggled to stay stable and on course. I kept my Nikon and its lenses handy to record the marvelous intricacies of rock, water, foliage, and sky as well as the faces of my companions, rock crevices, seals nosing our boat, pods of diving orcas, the little blue tents, the varied greens of grass and conifers. Every day a fresh revelation. Every day a deeper understanding of creation and Creator. Every day a fuller understanding of myself.

Every morning each of us would take an oar and fit it into the corresponding oarlock with one of our crew at the wooden tiller, keeping the little vessel on course. We learned rowing songs to keep the rhythm strong and steady—"Michael, Row the Boat Ashore," "Hey, Ho, Nobody at Home." Somehow, rowing together in rhythm joined us, body and spirit. We were a pack, an organism. As we rowed we relished our precision, raising our oars in vertical salutes to passing ferries. Even wearing rowing gloves our hands developed blisters, which we wore with pride. Our muscles ached but toughened with the effort of rowing against the tides.

One day, in order to reach our destination on a more distant island, we rowed for seventeen hours straight. This presented problems for certain limited bladders on board, but a bucket in the bow, with the rowers facing the stern, was available for relief, with a square of canvas available for "privacy." This was a bit much for one self-conscious graduate student who could only relieve himself by jumping overboard into the icy seawater. We soon hauled him in over the gunwale, dripping and nearly paralyzed with cold, having done his duty.

Near the end of the trip, we settled in a secluded bay on Saturna Island for two days, which allowed us the experience of individual solitude. Each of us found a site out of touch and hearing from the others where we could reflect and allow our bodies to catch up with our souls. I found a nook among the driftwood on the beach and felt kinship with the magnificent bones of the stranded tree trunks. The sun gleamed in and out. The only sound was the gentle wash of ripples on pebbles or, occasionally, the sharp cry of a Stellar jay. Butterflies drifted by. Ducks. I watched two otters playing in the shallows. I dreamed, wrote, read, meditated, felt a great inner peace and deep sense of connection with my surroundings. I was part of the created world, held in the Creator's love.

My world, inner and outer, had been both refocused and expanded. By putting myself into an unknown situation, I'd conquered anxiety about personal safety and comfort. My confidence had been renewed. At seventy-one, I felt ready for whatever God would next bring into my life.

Amy R. Buckley

Amy is a writer, speaker, and activist passionate about men and women reclaiming their truest, best selves in life together. She founded the Stop the Silence Initiative as an editor for shelovesmagazine.com, calling faith communities to bring justice and healing to those who have suffered abuse and violence. Amy has an MDiv and is a founding board member of Life Together International. She writes articles for a number of publications and blogs at amyrbuckley.com. Amy is a member of the Redbud Writers Guild.

Merging Branches

As a girl, I imagined someday falling in love and getting married. Having identified with fairy-tale heroines, I expected to meet and marry Prince Charming. We would buy a beautiful home, adopt a dog, and start a family. I envisioned walking down the aisle in an elegant white gown, dreaming of forever. I assumed marriage meant till death do us part. I never imagined my Prince Charming abruptly moving in with another woman a decade after our vows. I never thought my happy ending would also include the awkward, painful, and sometimes hilarious road of later-in-life dating and remarriage.

Shortly after my husband served me divorce papers, a seminary professor astutely commented, "Marriage is like the intertwining of two trees." Individuals have firmly planted roots, as well as branches that shoot upward and outward before they meet and merge with another person. When individuals merge in marriage, their own branches remain unique, but sometimes it's hard to tell which branches are which as they mysteriously braid and graft together. Dr. Catherine Clark Kroeger explained that when a partner dies, or chooses to disconnect, the remaining partner suffers unspeakable pain, confusion, and loss. Her branches have grown into particular shapes in relationship to her partner. Minus his presence, she faces a crisis: Who am I really? How can I continue without him? Will it ever be possible to merge myself with another?

I connected strongly with this metaphor. It seemed to really sum up the losses and confusion of my devastating new reality: divorcee.

After ten years of marriage, I didn't know how to disentangle myself from the *we*. Did I really like the dark coffee my former husband and I once drank together? Did I really enjoy hiking and canoeing? Was I really passionate about travel? As I emerged from the marriage and began to redefine myself, I also began to long for romantic companionship.

Dating later in life diverged significantly from my earlier experiences of moonlight and infatuation. I had a less-toned body and fewer fantasies of marital bliss. Marriage was a nut I had already cracked open. I had a history and habits and a life tied to a community. The prospect of intertwining branches with another person who had a different background and his own issues—what a perfect mess! More than a few times, I prayed, "Dear God, *really?*"

Not surprisingly, the pool of eligible dating partners shrinks after midlife. I didn't know even one bachelor looking for a mate. Among the throngs of people at church, there were very few singles in my age bracket. One kind person suggested her nephew as a candidate, and in the same breath hinted that I might "introduce him to Jesus" and "help him get his life together." I politely declined.

On a dare, I turned to online dating. But first, I consulted with my cousin, a professional marriage expert, on what I considered to be negotiable and nonnegotiable in marriage. He coached me in writing a profile based on those parameters. The Christian website I used enabled me to choose limits such as age and smoking or nonsmoking. I uploaded a recent photo and wrote that I was a master of divinity student with plans to work in ministry. I finally finished, hit send, and optimistically waited for potential matches.

First, I heard from "Joshua Seeks Proverbs 31 Woman." His description of the ideal wife sounded something like Mother Teresa meets a Victoria's Secret model. He did not mention what he would bring to a relationship. Delete. Second, I received a message from "Pete, the Communal Rancher." Although nice, he couldn't comprehend what I'd do with a master of divinity, and I couldn't see myself growing alfalfa and tending livestock. Delete. Then came "The Grey Goose." We spoke a few times by phone, and I learned his favorite movie was *It's a Wonderful Life*. A quick search revealed that he had lied considerably about his age. My psychologist cousin advised me to move on, saying, "Lying isn't negotiable ever, especially about a foundational issue."

My first round of online dating left me discouraged. As the realities of meeting someone compatible sank in, I canceled my online dating account and went back to making connections the old-fashioned way. "Don't worry, you'll meet someone," people I hardly knew commented, even a cashier in a grocery store. Did I look that desperate? Other kind souls—usually elderly women—whispered in my ears at church, "You should get married." I knew they meant well, but it wasn't as if I could run to Walmart and pick up a husband.

I reflected on my dating journey. Never-married men seemed more interested in "playing the field" than committing to a covenant relationship. Divorced men didn't seem healed enough to sustain a healthy relationship . . . not that I was perfect either. Then it dawned on me: I had not yet met a widower. I could not imagine having babies in my forties and the thought of meeting a man with children appealed to me. I couldn't bring myself to wish that a man would lose his wife, or some children would lose their mother, so I whispered, "Jesus, if there's already a man in that situation, and a couple of children who need a mom, I'd be glad for it." Something about that felt right.

After that prayer, I decided to give online dating a second chance. That's when I met Andrew and his two girls. In one photo, they were standing on a beach, smiling at the camera, ocean waters behind them. It impressed me how relaxed Andrew looked as the girls leaned on his legs. I later found out that they had gone to Hawaii for some respite after his wife had passed away from leukemia.

Andrew and I flew through questions relayed on the dating website. We advanced to speaking on the phone, covering topics from our favorite colors to personal stories, to faith and our hopes for the future. Conversations couldn't have been easier. The first time we met face-to-face was over breakfast at my home. He'd traveled all that way just for a weekend meeting. We picked at the eggs I'd nervously overcooked. They were cold when Andrew arrived, late because of a wrong turn.

I guess it all went well; we got engaged shortly after my seminary graduation. Six months after meeting, we exchanged vows in a private ceremony on the white sands of a mountain lake beach. I moved into Andrew's home, leaping from the professional world of theological education to the domestic realm of tending a home and stepmothering.

No amount of reading or advice could have prepared me for the realities of remarriage and a blended family in my forties. It's easier to conjugate Greek participles than to rebuild a family! I remember the first time the girls called me *Mommy;* I scanned the grocery store aisle looking for their mother before I realized, "Oh, that's me!"

The girls and I planted a garden that spring. It delighted us to watch sprouts of lettuce, tomatoes, carrots, and bright yellow marigolds poking through the soil. We carefully watered and weeded. We couldn't wait for the harvest. But one night, our rambunctious yellow Labrador broke into the garden; he gorged himself on the vegetables and trampled the flowers. The kids looked up at me sobbing, and I struggled to know what to say about their loss. But my struggles went far deeper: how do I help them process my presence as their "second mommy" after the loss of their "first mommy"?

"Seminary could not have prepared me for this," I often joke. Some days go better than others. We laugh, sob, and wonder how on earth it's even possible. Yet the Spirit of Jesus whispers and urges us forward: "Yes, I am the vine; you are the branches. Those who remain in me, and I in them, will produce much fruit. For apart from me you can do nothing" (John 15:5 NLT).

At forty-five, I've been a wife and mother now for six years. A folk sculpture of the Tree of Life hangs in our home near the front door. It serves as a reminder of the One who makes it possible for us—four different, wounded, flawed people—to rebuild our lives, together. We are far from figuring this out. Our branches twine together—and run amok, at times—in the messy, mysterious process of grafting together a beautiful new family.

Charity Singleton Craig

Charity is a writer of essays, stories, blog posts, and books. She is the coauthor of *On Being a Writer*, and she has contributed essays to three books, including *Letters to Me: Conversations with a Younger Self*. She is regularly published at *The Curator*, where she is a staff writer; *The High Calling*, where she is a content and copy editor; and TweetSpeak Poetry, where she is a contributing writer. She lives with her husband and three stepsons in central Indiana. You can find her online at charitysingletoncraig .com, on Twitter @charityscraig, and on Facebook.

This Is My Body

We are walking into church, my husband and I, and his hand on the small of my back feels normal now, like it belongs there. When the pastor prays, Steve grabs my hand. During the sermon, I feel his arm slide around me; my forearm rests on his thigh. When we get home, I kiss him as we both change clothes before making lunch.

These are our bodies, joined together, daring anyone who would to put them asunder. This is our marriage, an extended conversation of silent touches and brushes and caresses. This is the part no one ever told me about.

When I got married for the first time at age forty-two, only my best friend thought to prepare me for my wedding night. By then, I was expected to know. A rushed ceremony in light of an unexpected personal crisis meant only three friends and my dad attended. Our courtship had been brief; the engagement, briefer than expected because of this recurrent cancer diagnosis. Steve and I had greatly anticipated the consummation of our marriage; now my own body threatened our pleasure.

Books, movies, television—in a highly sexualized culture—had tutored me in the ways of men with women. My friend's brief advice and the knowledge of my own body filled in the gaps. Bodies older and wiser found a way on our wedding night. But the holy mystery of the union of two bodies wasn't revealed through the instruction of the media or a friend's advice for the honeymoon or even the limited self-awareness of a forty-two-year-old virgin. And four years later, I still shake my head and wonder as I feel my husband slip his arm around my waist.

~

About a year before my wedding—months before I even met Steve—that same best friend and I were talking on the phone about church. Our suburban congregation recently had built a new, larger sanctuary, and for many of us, the big topic of conversation revolved around where to sit. That week, my friend—a young widow—and I had found ourselves in the upper level, stage right, in a section filled with other single women who were all friends or friends of friends. Three rows deep we had sat, elbow to elbow with other women who were divorced or never married. During our phone conversation, my friend said she would rather not sit there again.

"I know," I told her, "the upper level was distracting."

"Yes, but no," she replied. "It's because of all the single women."

Tears formed in my eyes, and I resisted offense.

"That's my reality right now," I said.

"Mine, too," she replied. "But I don't want to be around only women, especially single women."

My heart burned as I recognized this same desire in myself. After a few difficult dating relationships in my twenties and a broken heart in my mid thirties, I had all but cut off men. Though I occasionally spent time with my friends' husbands and children, for the most part, I spent all my time both professionally and socially with women. And mostly *single* women.

Even though I was in my forties, had miraculously survived stage four cancer, and had grown pretty comfortable with my long-term singleness, I hadn't given up the idea that I might one day marry. It wasn't like I didn't know godly men full of integrity. I just didn't know how to have them in my life. Somehow, I had held onto my romantic notion of finding *the one and only* man of my dreams without ever intentionally being in the presence of men.

In the wisdom of Wendell Berry, I was trapped between the false notions of sexual romance and sexual capitalism.

As Berry explains it, sexual romance resists a "generality of instinct," seeking instead a soul mate, a one-of-a-kind match unlike any other man. Sexual capitalism, on the other hand, deals only in generalities, and sees all men "of a kind," particularly the disillusioned sexual romantic, who sees an ex-lover as representative of all worthless men. "But sexuality appears to be both general and particular," Berry contends. "One cannot love a particular woman [or man, in my case], for instance, unless one loves womankind—if not all women, at least other women."

Though I would not have expressed it this way at the time, my solution to this conundrum of sexual romance and sexual capitalism was to turn both fallacies on their heads by spending as much time with as many men as possible. Not by dating around, but instead, I joined groups only if they included both men and women. I was intentional about conversations with my dad, stepdad, and brothers. I paid closer attention to the few men I worked with, what they said and did. Assuming I would never marry, I set "happily ever after" aside and instead determined to see only the inherent value in all men.

Yet something was still missing. My approach had relegated me to a desexualized bodilessness. Since I had been grieving the absence of the "otherness" of men, in trying to exact a familiarity or "sameness," I remained lacking. In other words, simply replacing all my women friends with men didn't solve anything. But to embrace both the generality and particularly of my sexual identity meant I would have to come to terms with loving all men and loving one man at the same time. Could I do it?

When I was single, unmarried men were all fair game. A brush of his hand against my arm, his warmth as I stood next to him, a light embrace among friends—every touch was a sign to be interpreted. But the endless need for interpretation and the vast potential for mixed signals with single men paralyzed me. Thus, I had closed myself off.

At the same time, I held strictly to the code that men who were married were off limits to me. I was careful about physical proximity; I resisted being alone together; I would regularly inquire about a man's wife and children to keep always before us that there was no possible "we." These tight boundaries around married men somehow allowed me more freedom to be myself, which confused me.

It wasn't until I found myself surprisingly and miraculously married that I understood what others have probably always known about marriage: the vows aren't for the couple only. As Berry sees it, the vow of forsaking all others is made not only to a spouse but also to "all others." In this way, a marriage vow between one couple ushers them into a larger commitment of sexual responsibility to an entire community.

Of course, marriage didn't save me or complete me any more than it saves or completes any of us. Marriage was never intended for that. And as I shared at my bridal shower, marriage is not the best thing that ever happened to me, though I love my husband with all my heart. Jesus is. I still mention this to single friends who look at my specific marriage and gather hope for themselves.

But marriage as an institution helps us see a way forward as embodied people, especially in a culture that is far from sexually responsible. The vows of commitment and exclusivity serve as a reminder of both the freedom and the boundaries that exist in our relationships between men and women, whether single or married. This is how we all honor marriage and keep the marriage bed pure (Hebrews 13:4), even while acknowledging that marriage for some of our brothers and sisters is still an unattained longing, an undesirable encumbrance, or even a "gift" some would like to return.

"I hardly remember what my life used to be like," I often tell Steve when we talk about the years before we met. I spend most of my time now with men, or boys, cooking and cleaning and loving and laughing with my husband and three stepsons. This is my life now, and this is my body—my one scarred, aging body—given to one, and joined mysteriously to all.

Heather MacLaren Johnson

Heather is the mother of three children adopted from Russia, all with special needs. After adopting, Heather left her career as a clinical psychologist to focus on her children's needs. In midlife, she and her family moved to rural Wisconsin where they now run summer nature camps for at-risk, inner-city Milwaukee children, helping them learn about God through creation. Heather is a frequent corporate speaker for Great Marriages of Sheboygan County and a mentor for women at New Hope Pregnancy Center of Sheboygan, Wisconsin.

The Whole New World of Horses

I'm forty-seven and about to ride in my first dressage competition. I've only been riding a year and feel like an old mare who ain't what she used to be. But on this August afternoon, I'm sitting in a saddle on Liberty Belle, my black Morgan/quarter horse mare with a white star in the middle of her forehead. We're waiting our turn. She's antsy, eager to perform. I'm scared, wondering what in the world I'm doing here with other competitors twenty to thirty years younger than I am. My mouth is dry. The rest of me is sweaty, a combination of summer heat and frayed nerves.

Liberty Belle looks impeccable—showered and dried, brushed to a gleam, running braid in her mane. I'm properly attired—white shirt and stock tie secured with a gold pin; hip-length, black tailored jacket with gold buttons; white riding breeches tucked into tall black dressage boots; black leather gloves; and a black velvet riding helmet covering my mass of strawberry blond curls pulled back in a bun. I wish I felt as crisp and confident as my outfit portrayed. Truthfully, my anxiety is a nine out of ten. If I were a horse, I'd be bolting right about now.

I enter the ring where my trainer, Lacey, stands by the white fence, ready to call the riding pattern.

"Smile!" she tells me.

I take a deep breath, enter the ring, stop in the middle, face the panel of three judges, dip my chin in proper salute, and begin the pattern. Walk, trot, turn, stop. Trying to focus on the pattern, I'm thinking, *How in the world have I come here, a woman pushing fifty?*

The show results blare over the loudspeaker. My name is announced. Second place. Lacey, my trainer, is first place. Lacey reaches over and gives me a high five. I sit in my saddle, shocked. Me? An old mare? Second place? I thought back to the day I entered the whole new world of horses.

I was forty-two when my love of everything equine began. Our daughter, Anna, then ten, attended an equestrian day camp at a farm down the road from our home. Smitten with her assigned horse, Harley, Anna continued riding lessons after camp on another quarter horse named Chance. As I watched Anna, I thought she was born for the back of a horse, her brown hair flowing as the rest of her rocked in rhythm with Chance's canter.

For a girl with multiple challenges stemming from fetal exposure to alcohol and her first six years in a Russian orphanage, I was grateful for Anna's growing connection with Chance. I knew how a human–horse relationship can heal emotions and help with learning. I didn't know then how much God would use our new equine life to help me and so many others besides Anna.

After a year of lessons on Chance, we decided to lease a horse. Anna rode. I watched. We both learned together how to care for a horse completely and we both became strongly attached to this gentle mare named Faith. Then, a year later, Anna and I grieved.

Faith was stripped away from us. Without notice, Faith's owner moved her to a farm far away. Anna and I never had a chance to say goodbye to the horse we both loved. I wondered how this could happen. After praying, I thought perhaps broken hearts can create open hearts for God's greater good, where bigger dreams can come true. Perhaps our loss of Faith was exactly what we needed to propel us forward to see the greatness of God's hand at work in our lives and in the lives of others.

The loss of Faith led us to a neglected horse in need of a nurturing new home. At first, I was hesitant about the Appaloosa named Roscoe because of his size. Anna, five feet tall and ninety-five pounds, compared with Roscoe, sixteen hands, tall in comparison to most other horses, seemed like a misfit. But as I watched Anna ride Roscoe around the arena—this horse who had been wounded—I saw a perfect fit for our daughter. I wrote a check that day and became a first-time horse owner at forty-four and Anna began her nightly prayers that we would move to a farm so Roscoe could live with us. I never believed we would ever move to the country, let alone a horse farm. My husband and I were suburban through and through and knew nothing other than subdivision living.

A year later, after receiving the sky-high quote for an addition to our home we desperately needed, I found myself searching the internet for other possibilities. Up came a property. I knew its exact location—directly west of good friends who owned a summer cottage on Lake Michigan, thirty minutes north of us and ten minutes south of our own Lake Michigan cottage.

The home was set on forty-four acres of meadows and ponds, willows and pines. I showed the listing to Todd. He stated emphatically, "We're not moving." I nodded. Then, I secretly set an appointment with the real estate agent to view the property alone. After the showing, I told Todd I had just toured the property of his dreams.

Two days later, Todd and I drove up the long gravel drive and met the agent at the front door of the log home. We walked in and around. Todd said not one single word. Then, at the end of the tour, he asked, "Where do the trails start?"

We meandered around the property alone, spotting a red-tailed hawk perched on an oak branch and a pair of Sandhill cranes warbling in the blue sky. Todd remained silent until we completed our hike. Then, standing in the center of the back yard facing west, he wrapped his arm around me. "Can you see us growing old together here?" I smiled, seeing a "SOLD" sign in my mind.

Two months later, Anna's prayer had been answered affirmatively. We became country folks and I began climbing the steepest learning curve of my life. While Todd researched and purchased a farm-sized tractor, I designed a barn and hired a builder. Our family fenced pastures and the outdoor riding arena. I learned how to compost the ton of manure we were about to accumulate annually. When all was nearly done, I learned Roscoe would need another four-legged companion. At age forty-five, I decided it might be good to get off the ground and into my own saddle.

Our trainer found the perfect match for me. "She's more horse than you can handle right now, but she's smart and talented. She'll teach you to ride." Frankly, I thought I'd rather learn from a human, but I trusted Lacey's judgment and bought that horse I named Liberty Belle. Turns out, that horse was exactly what this middle-aged woman needed to be set free from her fears.

Over the next year, that smart but bossy mare did teach me to ride. After a few naughty shoulder-in maneuvers that flipped me off her back and onto hard ground, I got smart and stubborn, deciding I would never get dumped by a horse again. I learned to anticipate Libby's moves and became an accomplished equestrian.

Though I thought I'd faint from nerves during our first competition, Libby lit up the ring and helped me place second, surpassed only by Lacey who just happened to be riding the third horse I had added to our herd that year, an Arabian/paint named Shania, a rescue horse we adopted.

We've been here on the farm for more than a decade since that dressage competition. Every summer, dozens of high-risk youth from the heart of Milwaukee come for a day-camp we run. They strap on helmets and ride our horses. They see and learn about caterpillars munching milkweed, spinning and pushing through their chrysalises, becoming vibrant orange-and-black monarchs feeding on our purple meadow asters. The camp kids squeal as they dig their little hands into what was once horse waste, now sweet-smelling soil, transformed by heaven's rain, sun's warmth, and the regular tossing and turning that keep it cooking until ready to feed all our flowers, vegetables, fruit trees, and hayfields that feed us humans, horses, and so many others.

Our kids are now grown but still call our farm home—the place we come together each Sunday for hikes and trail rides, for celebrating adoption of humans and horses, for feeling the wooing of God in the wild and the wind. We pass the place where we buried our first family dog, Isabelle, up on the hill, where we set a white cross in the earth as we all stood in a circle, holding hands in prayer. As I see that cross today, I offer silent prayers of thanks that this now fifty-seven-year-old "mare" is more than she used to be, thanks to our challenged daughter who prayed her family and her horse all the way to this country cathedral where God meets many and showers his amazing grace.

Elisa Morgan

Elisa was named by *Christianity Today* as one of the top fifty women influencing today's church and culture. Her many books include *The Beauty of Broken, She Did What She Could, The NIV Mom's Devotional Bible*, and *Hello, Beauty Full: Seeing Yourself As God Sees You.* For twenty years, Elisa served as CEO of MOPS International. She speaks internationally and serves as a cohost of the syndicated radio program *Discover the Word.* With her husband of thirty-five years, Evan, she has two grown children and two grandchildren who live near her in Denver, Colorado.

Something BIG

I wanted something *big* to do. And just maybe something I'd never done before.

After twenty years as CEO of an international ministry—day in, day out leading an effort that swept me under the wake of its growth more than once—I found a welcome slowing and then gradually . . . a restless inertia. Yes, I recognized some never-before-present parameters in my closer-to-retirement days. But I wasn't retiring. I wasn't old enough. I was doing something a bit less necessary and quite different, but I was still fully active. My energy whirled in expectancy until I realized I had extra time on my hands.

Mercy, you say, *really? Give me some! Who has* time *on their hands?*
I did.

Well, not lots—not hours or days or even predictable thirty-minute slots. I still traveled to various speaking engagements, kept up with a zillion emails, picked up my then five-and-a-half-year-old grandson at kindergarten and squished Play-Doh into snakes and pasta and meat-balls on my kitchen island. I did the laundry and cleaned out files and met friends for mentoring—both for them and for me. I began writing a manuscript for a personal memoir.

But there was something *missing* inside me. What else did others do in this crinkling orange season of their lives? Every time I peered into the hollow hole to investigate it further—you know to like say, "God where are you going to call me next and just exactly when?" I'd get a still, small voice response along the lines of *Chill, Elisa.*

Chill. Right.

I wanted something big to do.

So I listened to an urge that had begun to grow louder each month. It had first appeared the prior spring when I was caring for my adult son's ninety-pound Rottweiler, Darla. Yep. Ninety pounds. (I weigh about one hundred ten. Shut up—it's genetic. I take no credit whatsoever.)

At this midpoint in my life, I didn't even *like* dogs. Dogs bite me. I don't know why, but they always have and still do. I'd never had a dog of my own. Growing up, we'd had two dogs in our home—a fluffy black cocker spaniel appropriately named Lacey and a hyperactive American Eskimo christened "Martini with a Twist" on account of her tail that corkscrewed over her rear end. And because my mom loved cocktails and thought that was a name to die for. But neither of those dogs was mine.

In a motherly moment when I agreed to help out my adult son, Darla came to live with my husband, Evan, and me for several months. She wolfed down dog food in our laundry room and pranced around in her rhinestone-encrusted pink leather collar. She insistently nudged my elbow while I typed at my keyboard. I'd find myself smooching and petting her for minutes on end.

After a few weeks, I'd wake to the sound of my dear husband cooing, "Good girl" through the wires of her crate, releasing her to stretch and yawn and then cajoling her to stillness while he fastened her "jewelry" in place. We were besotted.

Every day—in my new work wardrobe of pajamas or workout clothes—I'd eye the clock and arrange my phone appointments until it was mid afternoon when Darla would magically appear, insistently nudging my elbow from my keyboard, demanding attention. It was time to head out for our walk in the wild behind our house. When we hit the grass, I'd let her off the leash and watch with a strange contentment as she ran, free and happy.

One late afternoon as I returned, I was focused on my life—or lack of one—and my eyes scanned only the ground beneath my feet. Darla was back on her leash, happily prancing at my side. I looked up just at the last second to see two enormous Akitas hurtling toward me—off their leashes. There was no human companion in sight. Darla froze. So did I. In seconds, the Akitas pounced on Darla. Instinctively, I railed up like a giant grizzly and screamed for them to *get off!* One of the dogs bit my leg, then ran for the bushes. Stunned and shaken, Darla and I turned to each other and examined our wounds. We were both bleeding but all right and limped home where we nuzzled each other like two siblings. What was it that formed in this shared wounding?

When it was time for Darla to return to my son, I found it surprisingly hard to let her go. She had brought something meaningful, distracting, joyful, and big into my days. Her absence tore a hole in my life.

When I completed my fall speaking schedule and looked at the yawning weeks of home work—back at my computer—I made a decision. Clear that I was supposed to continue in the work where God had placed me, in a season of a quieter life, I went hunting.

I came home with a rottie-wannabe. I named him Wilson because his favorite thing in life, besides me, was a tennis ball. He was three years old, a rottweiler/Labrador/shepherd mix. He weighed about seventy-five pounds, but I think if you would have asked him, he would have completely denied his size. Our nightly ritual included me on the carpet, back against the bedframe, and Wilson fetaled at my side, curled like a purse puppy into the space under my arm. He was the very first dog that ever owned me. And he was big enough.

As life would have it, three weeks after Wilson became mine, Darla returned—this time for good. My son needed to move on from the responsibility of a dog and Evan and I were . . . well, undeniably bonded as grand-dog parents.

We now have two crates. Two leashes. Two collars—one pink and sparkly and one camo. Each morning I shovel kibble into the dogs' bowls, spoon out powdered hip/joint supplement, inject insulin, and pop a Rimadyl into Darla's diabetic body. I work to offer equal nuzzles and smooches. Fairness reigns in my new dog-mom role.

My friends marvel at my transformation from bitten to smitten. My son beams at my conversion to his side of the dog park. My husband looks at me over the black/brown heads of our dogs and smiles; we have in some ways returned to thirty years ago when we exchanged proud glances over the tops of our toddlers' heads.

Oddly, I can barely recall the old inner cringe that would grab me when passing an unknown dog on my solo walks. The fear of being devoured seems the very soil where love has dug in a new root of meaning. Of relationship. Of belonging.

Somehow God knew this. This buried-like-a-bone need in me, that I would one day scratch to the surface, grab in my teeth, shake, and refuse to relinquish. Something big. Something new. Something that would never be undone.

Sheila Wise Rowe

Sheila is passionate about helping people to grow more in love with Jesus and heal from past hurts. Sheila has a master's degree in counseling and over twenty-five years of experience as a Christian counselor, missionary, writer, teacher, and artist in America, France, and South Africa. She is a member of the Redbud Writer's Guild and coauthor of *The Well of Life*. Sheila is happily married to Dr. Nicholas Rowe and is the mother of two delightful college students. Visit therehobothhouse.com or follow The Well of Life Book on Facebook.

Awakened to Adventure

At forty-two, my life was a well-choreographed dance. Every morning was a sprint to get everyone out the door. Days were spent counseling women and couples in distress. Afternoons I jogged up the street just as our kids stepped off the school bus. Weekends consisted of occasional date nights, school events, soccer practices, and church.

At midlife, I'd settled into a routine. Like many other women, I felt in some ways like my life was over. But God was about to awaken me with a challenge. One night, I watched a TV special on the impact of HIV/AIDS in Africa. I cried through it, pleading with God to do something. He said he would, and I would be part of his plan.

The following year—at the age of forty-three—I went on my first ever mission trip, to the country of South Africa. It took eighteen hours of flying to reach Johannesburg, where our small group joined a ministry team at the HIV/AIDS and Emotional Healing Conference. We listened, shared stories, and prayed with people as they processed their pain. Later, while visiting an orphanage, my heart broke as I prayed for the babies orphaned by AIDS.

On the last day, we celebrated at the Pilanesberg National Park and Game Reserve. We viewed lions, giraffes, and elephants among rugged hills, grassy plains, and an unobstructed sky. In this stunning beauty, I felt a profound sense of Jesus's heart for South Africa. I left Johannesburg both depleted and exhilarated by my encounters, with a prompting in my heart: *One day you will return.*

I've always been a risk taker, but I wasn't sure about returning. I spent four years counting the costs while grappling with the call and the decision. I was forty-six years old when I finally said yes. I would work with Emthonjeni, an HIV/AIDS project located in an informal settlement. My husband would work with The Evangelical Alliance of South Africa. As the school year came to a close, our kids, ages eight and eleven, were tearful about the move. Our extended family was resigned, but we were resolved. That June, we boarded a plane as full-time missionaries to South Africa.

South Africa is known as the Rainbow Nation, a complex multi-ethnic culture still working through the racial divisions of the past. Johannesburg, our new home, set in the northwestern interior, was a beautiful city. Despite its size, nearly four million residents, it boasts the world's largest man-made urban forest with over six million trees. The entire city lies under a lush green canopy.

To be an African American woman in a country with a black majority felt in some ways like I had finally come home. But people assumed I spoke Zulu and my attempts to speak it mostly resulted in confusion or laughter. Our new church mirrored the complexion of the nation—a multicultural community of mostly college-age and young adults. I saw deep relationships forming between ethnically different believers.

Not long after we arrived, a large house was offered to our church for ministry, and I founded Malibongwe—May His Name Be Praised—a transitional home for abused and homeless mothers and their children. Along with our project assistant, Janine, and live-in house mothers MaGlenda and MaJabu, we opened Malibongwe with prayer and thanksgiving. Lebo and her two children were the first occupants. They had been homeless, begging on the streets, and sleeping in the catacombs of a local cemetery. Within two weeks there were five women and six children, each carrying their own deep hurts.

The women accepted Christ while simultaneously struggling with pressure from relatives; past and prospective lovers tried to lure them to return to their old lives. Busi, a teenager, was abducted en route to meet old friends. Her sister was distraught as we tried to retrace Busi's last steps, to no avail. We prayed desperately for her safe return. After two weeks Busi escaped her captors, and we learned of the abuse she had endured. We went to file a police report only to be shamed and interrogated. Worst of all, Busi's abductors knew where she lived. I was angry and afraid for the safety of us all.

Over the next two years, we continued to share the Word and our lives together; we all grew spiritually, healed emotionally, and began to dream again. I watched the children become carefree. Lebo's youngest no longer hoarded food or begged money from the neighbors. Each morning their squeals greeted me—"Mom Sheila! Mom Sheila!"—with hugs all around. Despite its success, after three years with increased overhead and dwindling donors, Malibongwe closed. It was such an enormous loss, I began to question everything.

One day the Lord told me I was at a crossroads. Like a driver of a car who focuses on a roadside tree and not on the road ahead, my faith would drift toward wherever my eyes were fixed. If I continued to focus on what others could have or should have done rather than what God did and was doing, I'd crash.

I released the pain, disappointment, and unforgiveness that I built around my own heart. At fifty-one, I was learning that maturity involves living with unmet needs and unanswered questions. I began to realize that in beauty or in tragedy, God alone is in control. He is the source of my real security.

As the psalmist exclaims, "LORD, you alone are my portion and my cup; you make my lot secure. The boundary lines have fallen for me in pleasant places; surely I have a delightful inheritance" (Psalm 16:5–6).

The Lord gave me five more years of ministry, leading Rebecca's Well projects, a fruitful outreach program for teenage girls and women in the townships. Then in August 2015, after almost eleven years, the Lord released us to return to America.

Our farewell party was held at the church. I was overwhelmed by those who came to celebrate with us and wept as they gave testimony. Lebo's sixteen-year-old daughter stood up and said, "I am not supposed to be here," as she recounted the day she and her mom and little sister had wandered in from the cold. She now dreams of becoming an attorney.

Jolly, a board member, pointed to the carved elephant letter openers she had placed on each table. "For most Africans, the king of the jungle is not the lion; it is the elephant, Ndlovu. Elephants are a keystone species; their role is so significant that their removal causes dramatic shifts in ecosystems. Here in South Africa if your last name is Ndlovu, it's likely you have a royal heritage. Sheila, although you were not born in Africa, you are African in every way. God is pleased with you and what you have done. He has renamed you; your surname is now Ndlovu."

Eleven years ago, I'd been afraid to follow God. I thought my days of adventure were over. Now at fifty-six and looking back, I see how God patiently and faithfully called me. Even when my faith was low and my protective walls were high, he carried and kept me. I know the risk I took was well worth it, and many more adventures await as I follow the Lord!

Amy K. Sorrells

Amy's diverse writing career spans over two decades of freelance writing, including medical journal publications, novels, and a popular op-ed newspaper column. Praised by reviewers for the way they both poetically and accurately portray real-life hardship and hope, Amy's novels, including *How Sweet the Sound* and *Lead Me Home*, are inspired by social issues that break her heart and the Bible stories that reflect God's response to those issues. A practicing registered nurse, she lives in central Indiana with her husband and three sons.

My Body, My Fixer-Upper

I've been mad about being in my forties for six years. It might be about time I get over it.

The problem is, everything my over-forty friends warned me about keeps coming true. I threw my back out running a vacuum. Some days I can't remember my children's names. I gain weight if I so much as look at a cookie.

The height of my despair came when I stepped on the scale a year ago and realized the number on it was the same number as when I was nine months pregnant with my first child.

This time I didn't have pregnancy to blame.

It wasn't just the weight. I was plagued with abdominal pains, or "intestinal spasms" as my doctor called them. My migraines had escalated to the point that the left side of my face and my arm went numb. I felt so fatigued that I spent much of the day in bed sleeping after my kids went to school. When I finally dragged myself to a neurologist, he was so concerned about my symptoms that he ran a series of tests to rule out multiple sclerosis.

What's wrong with me, Lord? I prayed. Lamented.

I'd been a collegiate swimmer. People used to make fun of me for being too skinny. I used to be able to eat whatever I wanted. Not only did I not feel like myself anymore, I didn't look like myself either.

Thankfully, the multiple sclerosis tests came back negative, but the migraines and seemingly uncontrollable weight gain persisted. And so did my misery. I felt like I'd let myself down; I'd let my husband down (although he has never gone a day without telling me he thinks I'm beautiful), and God as well.

"Your body is a temple of the Holy Spirit," kept rolling around the back of my mind, but one look in the mirror indicated my temple needed an overhaul the likes of a *Fixer Upper* episode. I wanted to give up. I had no idea how I'd ever stop feeling fatigued, or how to stop gaining weight. But when I looked at my husband and my sons, and when I considered that the Lord still has Jeremiah 29:11 plans even for pitiful old me, I gathered up enough gumption to begin.

The first step in my journey toward wellness was making an appointment with my doctor. I felt so ashamed on my first visit when I stepped on the scale and saw that number again. I'd never needed help with my weight. But my doctor quickly assuaged my anxiety with kindness and reassurance. He explained the changes that were happening in my body. I learned the scary phrase "sarcopenia of aging" and the more obvious "metabolic syndrome." Both of these are fancy phrases for the ways our body slows its processing of food and the gradual breakdown of muscles. The changes often begin around the age of—you guessed it— forty. We become prone to falls and can experience weakened bones, weight gain, chronic pain, inflammation-related disorders, arthritis, and migraines.

The good news is, doctors and scientists are discovering that a combination of diet and exercise can prevent and even reduce these deteriorations. Add prayer to the mix, and you may discover, like I have, that you don't have to become captive to a body that doesn't feel like your own!

The first thing I had to change was my activity level. Developing muscle strength is one key to helping reduce these over-forty body changes. In the scientific journal *Applied Physiology, Nutrition, and Metabolism,*

Adam Johnston and his colleagues wrote, "Skeletal muscle aging is associated with a significant loss of muscle mass, strength, function, and quality of life. . . . It is also quite clear that regular resistance exercise is a potent and effective countermeasure for skeletal muscle aging."[1]

Eureka! All I needed to do was lift a few weights! I bounded to the gym and enthusiastically signed up with a personal trainer. That first session, he put me through a series of resistance exercises that caused me to almost pass out. I had to sit down in the middle of the gym, with svelte and toned young women wearing spandex all around me, as I fought stars and blackness. I swear I heard them all laughing.

Tail between my aching legs, I went back to the doctor. He kindly told me I couldn't exercise like I'm twenty anymore. I eventually learned how to do resistance training correctly, slowly building up repetitions with weight machines and doing exercises like squats, planks, and leg raises. I got myself back in the swimming pool. When it's sunny and above thirty degrees outside, I walk my dogs. We are never too old to get our body moving.

The second lifestyle adjustment was my diet. I discovered, through a simple elimination diet, that my abdominal cramps were the result of a lactose intolerance—something many people acquire as they age. This was by far the most difficult news of my journey back to wellness. I threw my fist up at the Lord over this one. Why couldn't I have been chocolate intolerant instead! I love milk! I crave big glasses of milk at bedtime and cheese and sour cream on everything. Even so, I swallowed hard and quit dairy. And not just dairy, but I quit diet drinks. I quit caffeine. I quit processed food.

I downloaded an app on my phone that allows me to count my calories. I added foods high in protein. I still struggle with getting green leafy foods down, but I try. And sometimes I cheat.

I've learned that lactose, processed foods, and artificial sweeteners are everywhere in our Western diets. They can cause inflammatory conditions such as migraines and chronic pain. Combine this with the fact that our metabolism needs all the help it can get after forty, and it makes sense that eating a cleaner and more natural diet is important for our bodies.

Sometimes I want a giant bowlful of fettucine alfredo so badly, and I order one from my favorite local Italian restaurant. But as with exercise, moderation is the key.

Aging isn't easy. Changing my lifestyle hasn't been easy either. But I've lost thirty pounds. I don't crawl back into bed in the mornings anymore. And I can't remember the last time I had a migraine.

The Lord says, "Exercise daily in God—no spiritual flabbiness, please! Workouts in the gymnasium are useful, but a disciplined life in God is far more so, making you fit both today and forever" (1 Timothy 4:7–8 MSG).

The Lord is the one who knows us inside and out. He gave us food and bodies that move, and he knows that in a broken world, food and bodies are often broken too. And yet, he never leaves us. He wants to help us. He longs for us to live full and joyful lives.

I'm learning to be less ticked off about being over forty. Without this struggle, I might not have known the sweetness of the Lord showing himself strong and faithful and kind in the midst of it. He put a doctor and encouraging friends and others in my path who helped me find a way to regain wellness in my life. He can do the same for you. Wrinkles and stretch marks and a few extra curves are badges of honor. And while I don't have to look like a goddess, maintaining my body is a spiritual discipline that allows me the privilege of living more fully for him.

Notes

1. Adam P. W. Johnston, Michael De Lisio, and Gianni Parise, "Resistance Training, Sarcopenia, and the Mitochondrial Theory of Aging," *Applied Physiology, Nutrition, and Metabolism* 33, no. 1 (February 2008): 191–99, doi: 10.1139/H07-141.

Leslie Leyland Fields

Leslie has birthed six kids, eleven books, three houses (yes, building a house is a kind of birth!), and an annual writer's workshop (the Harvester Island Wilderness Workshop). The year this book releases, she'll be in the midst of eight months of travel throughout Europe and South Africa with her husband and two youngest sons, teaching and sharing her serious pursuit of joy and praise. When she turns eighty, she plans to buy another scandalous bra.

❧

My First Padded Bra

The year I was turning fifty I had plans. Big plans. I was going to get my first manicure. I was going to run my first marathon. I was going to climb Mt. Kilimanjaro with Joni on her fiftieth birthday. Then my hips and joints started getting cranky. My budget for international travel seized up. I forgot about the manicure. Instead, I had a party with fifty friends. And after that, I did it. I bought my first padded bra.

I'm not exactly sure how it happened. It wasn't premeditated. I was traveling and ended up in a department store, slinking undercover through the lingerie section. Then—lightbulb flash. With a sexy little something, I could repay my husband for being Mr. Mom the week I was away. The padded bras beckoned—objects of both fascination and repulsion. They looked like foamy dishes and came in an astounding range of sizes, from little teacups to Italian restaurant–worthy bowls. But alas, no size was my size. Even batteries come in AAA! (How is it that the sizing is the same as for batteries, anyway?) Then on a little end rack, I found it. A flirty, spongy little number that looked small enough to fit.

I've worn sports bras most of my life. I've never worn fitted bras, only the stretchy fill-as-you-can kind. I've felt their power all these years. No matter what I was wearing on the outside, underneath I felt sporty, ready to break into a jog or an aerobic routine at any moment. And often I did. My bra inspired me. I've always taken pleasure in my boyishness and the freedom it brought. I've felt like Peter Pan refusing to grow up, my chest proof I was still young, nubile, and mobile.

Despite our culture's unflagging obsession with breasts, I've never felt insecure about mine. They may be less decorative than others', but few have enjoyed the same utility. Mine have fed people—six, actually—growing them from mewling newborn to stalwart near-toddler. A full six years logged on these breasts, boosting closeness, intelligence, and immunity for us both, a whole string of benefits conferred from my milk-rich low-fat deposits.

But during my freshman year of high school I would have traded with anyone. Breasts were so much in demand that year that tissue-stuffed bras became something of a norm, a trend I joined while hoping for nature to take its usual hormonal course. I soon gave up on the venture, especially after the tissues crept unbidden out of my shirt one day in plain view of the boy I had a crush on. When I saw his eye wander downward, I should have simply yanked out a tissue with a flourish and blown my suddenly stuffy nose, winking seductively like, "Aren't we girls inventive creatures who can stow the most necessary items in such mystical places?"

I do recall a few other moments in college, when I layered a second bra over my first, aiming for some kind of collegial shape to my body. I wanted to at least belong among the freshman femininity parading before the male upperclassmen, whom we knew were surveying the goods as we clicked by on our heels, swishing our skirts. (Yes, we wore high heels and skirts. Modest, of course. This was a Christian college where "the men looked like men and the women looked like women"—a great obsession of conservative Christians in the unisex hippie days of flowing hair, platform shoes, and patched jeans.)

I'm happy to report as well that this new bra, all foamy and thick, plush in just the right places, was not a tame bra; it was leopard-spotted. It made me feel a little wild. I wore it nearly every day. I was not making any kind of statement. I wore it so no one would notice me. So if anyone thought to comment on my new look, they might say, "There's a middle-aged woman in a polka-dot blouse," instead of, "There's a middle-aged woman without any breasts."

I look better in my clothes, I discovered—after all these years. My blouses don't bag in the front. My waist looks slightly smaller (a new interest with menopause setting in). I like it. For the first time since my nursing days, I am thinking that breasts are a good idea. Maybe God knew something here. I'm happy to be able to strap some breasts on when I want them.

And I'm also relieved to take them off.

I think I'm beginning to understand why women want breasts. Most women have them anyway, and since it's one of the major ways we're distinguished from men, why not celebrate and even exaggerate the distinction? Why not dress to highlight the obvious? (But then, that next step, why not have my body cut open to insert little baggies of salt water or silicone? No.)

I'm not a total dunce. I know it's about power and sex—all that. I remember that kind of power. In my twenties and thirties, when I traveled alone, men would try to flirt with me (me, in my rubber band bra), angling for a number, whatever they could extract. I never played. They were so pathetically obvious, and I was clearly ring-on-the-finger married and uninterested. Still, looking back, it was flattering.

Maybe I'm fooling myself now and really just want some of that power back. Aging is about as much fun as I anticipated twenty or so years ago. And I'm not sure women are getting much help. Women's magazines could do better. I'm a sucker for inspirational articles: makeup makeovers, wardrobe do-overs, hair fix-its, fat-to-thin befores and afters. But on the "older woman" front, I'm continually disappointed. Invariably the magazines feature women in their forties, fifties, and sixties who are still knockouts. "Look! You may be older, but you can still be gorgeous!" is the message. But these chosen ones, who look better at sixty than most of us looked at twenty, were, first of all, born gorgeous, and second, much of their current look comes via airbrushing, implants, surgeries, lipo, lasers, and tucks, to name just a few interventions. Is this the best we can do? This summarily dumps us all back into ninth grade. Are we still coining our value on our looks? Have we learned nothing in the decades since?

Movies aren't much better. In an older movie I watched again recently, a twenty-eight-year-old guy falls for Michelle Pfeiffer, who's twenty years older. Of course he falls for her. She's the craziest-beautiful fifty-year-old woman I've ever seen (and the craziest-beautiful forty-year-old, thirty-year-old, you get my drift). Of course he doesn't notice her age—she doesn't look her age! (What if she did? What if she were thirty pounds heavier—the size of a normal fifty-year-old, that is? What if she didn't have those lips, those hips?) The whole setup is patently unfair and does not, I repeat to well-meaning moviemakers, *does not* inspire older women to believe in themselves.

And I hope I never see another article on Tina Turner, who was eternally famous for her unending, incredibly toned legs, usually festooned in fishnets and exposed nearly all the way up. And she is nearing seventy in those photos. Yes, it's incredible. Yes, Tina Turner, you have fabulous legs, better than any *fifty*-year-old I know. Congratulations, you lucky woman, you. Now what? We put the magazine down and avoid the mirror. We end up believing the same old message from high school: If you've got it, you're a player. If not, game over.

Last month, I spent some time with a friend from college. We're the same age. She's had breast implants, Botox, an eye lift, full facial laser treatment, a fat transfer, and I don't know what else. She's also much thinner than I am and dresses like a Vogue cover girl. She looks fantastic. When I'm with her, I'm invisible. Everyone rubbernecks—men, women, children. I watch them watch her—relieved, actually.

I love her a lot, but—I recently realized—I don't want to be her. I don't want to be that noticed.

I've come to some other realizations lately, inspired by the new decade I'm wearing. I'm trying to feel good about myself and my increasingly visible changes, but feeling good isn't enough. I read an article in a semi-religious digest last month that instructed women to start their day by standing in front of the mirror, wrapping their arms around themselves, and reciting, "I love you! You're so beautiful!" as many times as they needed, an unabashed hail-to-the-self.

Surely there's more to feeling good about ourselves than feeling good about ourselves. I think there is. I see it on the faces of a few women I know in their seventies and eighties, women with wide waists, sagging chests, and creased, smiling faces, faces brightly turned to others. These are women who feel good about themselves, but clearly, they feel even better about others.

Truth be told, I might envy Michelle Pfeiffer and the other menopausal women who look so great, but I'm saving my admiration for the women who truly are great. Who are so busy being themselves and doing good work at home and out in the world, they don't have the time or the interest to worry about their wrinkles or their bustline. I see some of these women at my local coffee shop, at church, at a local nursing home, in the hospital waiting room. Women who love others completely, with abandon. No one's taking their picture. (They're almost invisible—at first.)

I'm not one of them. Not yet anyway. My vanity still props me against the mirror every morning, massaging high-promise creams into the latest creases and lines. I'm always trying to lose ten pounds. I wear shocking red lipstick, splurge occasionally on a froufrou coat, fret about my varicose veins. I still want to feel and look good. But more than that—and more than ever—I want to be good. I want to be the kind of person who sees beyond herself to others around her. The kind who loves her neighbor like herself, who does for others what she would like others to do for her, two golden rules that never show their age. When I see others doing this, it's so beautiful, it takes my breath away.

I'm trying to practice this now, some days in my padded bra. But I may not wear it forever. Ten or twenty years from now, maybe I'll be back to my sports bra. If anyone should notice me in a coffee shop, church, or hospital, leaning toward others in laughter, in friendship, in service, maybe they'll say, "Look at that happy old woman in that red lipstick and polka-dot blouse."

Or maybe, older and wiser themselves, they'll simply say, "Look at that woman over there. Isn't she beautiful?"

Lasts

Every new beginning comes from another beginning's end.
SENECA

*For one, dazzling, infinite moment, August felt like he
was standing on a precipice, the end of one world and the
beginning of another, a whisper and a bang.*
VICTORIA SCHWAB, *THIS SAVAGE SONG*

We're two weeks into the commercial salmon season off our island in Alaska. I'm excited. I'm going out tonight in the skiff, an open twenty-six-foot aluminum boat, with two of my sons, Elisha and Micah, twenty and twelve. I've not fished with Elisha since I don't know when. I am not any of my sons' preferred crewman, being of lesser weight, strength, and length than their usual crew, all of whom are in their twenties. Long arms and weight-lifting biceps are a decided advantage when leaning out of the skiff to snatch the net and pull it up into the boat, all while in motion. Though I'm only five feet, two inches tall, I'm agile and experienced. I just want to work, get wet, handle fish, and be with my sons, who spend most of their time in the fishing boats.

But maybe I picked the wrong night. Two hours into our work on the ocean, the wind comes up. The sea stirs, making our work much harder. Micah and I are focused on the line work, on moving the gear down the skiff, on "popping" the buoys. The lines are all rigid-tight now, the boat is carpeted in kelp, making every move slippery, and the skiff itself is pitching both side to side and front and back. Nothing happens now without careful intent and measurement. Where you step, how fast, grabbing the line, tossing the fish—the labor is immediately doubled. By the time we finish this net, the fun is long gone and my stomach is beginning to roil.

On the next net, the seas increase. We're taking on spray now as the tops of some of the waves curl and break into the stern. We cannot talk for the howl of the wind in our ears. It has only been three hours, but my arms are turning to rubber and my hands no longer want to grab. Elisha yells for me to catch the net. I try and cannot. It takes us three tries to get it.

I am working with gritted teeth now, willing my body to obey, to hold the lines tight, to pull on the sway buoy, but I am not doing well. My intent is to help, and I am not much help in this weather. I feel badly for Elisha, who is out in this blow with me instead of with a young, muscled crewman. I am not afraid of work or given to fear, and I've always been stronger than my peers, but who am I fooling? I'm almost sixty. It's not fair to Elisha and Micah. It's clear I have to make a decision. I either have to get back in full strength—lifting weights—or decide that I'm done going out in the boat. At least in storms. I know what I need to do. I feel a weight fall from my shoulders and a twinge of relief. I don't have to prove myself anymore, like I did years ago when I first came out here. I don't have to be as strong and as tough as the men. I can just let all that go. Though the skiff is still pitching beneath me and there is one long net to go, I suddenly stand full height, feeling lighter and ten years younger.

Just as we are embracing and enlarging our lives with new adventures and experiences, we're making room for new identities by letting go of what we no longer need. The years bring discernment, laughter, and a thrilling kind of honesty that allows us to peel off every weight that slows us down, as the apostle Paul admonishes us (Hebrews 12:1). Each of us in this section, then, present with enthusiasm our lasts, which we could also call our let-it-gos.

In these next chapters, you will meet **Shelly Wildman**, who will make you laugh out loud as she rejoices in the end of her monthly "curse"!

Jeanne Murray Walker, after a startling encounter with road rage and a homeless woman, realizes it's about time she gives up her judgments. Of course, we're all dealing with body issues through these middle years. **Andrea Stephens** finally and beautifully reckons with the reality that she will never bear children. Our youth-obsessed culture gets a smart send-up from **Margot Starbuck,** who dishes about swimsuits, jiggly thighs, and the Jesus-way to love her body. **Nancy Stafford,** beauty queen and award-winning actress, wryly writes of using Botox while hosting a TV show on natural living.

What else do we need to peel from our lives? What about failure, busyness, regret, envy? **Shannon Ethridge** turns a pink-slip moment into the beginnings of a new ministry. **Amy F. Davis Abdallah,** once a world traveler and now with a baby and toddler under foot, banishes her pining for independence as she embraces the limits of freedom. When **Michelle Van Loon** falls apart in a restaurant with her embarrassed teens, she finally begins to let go of a decades-long regret. In her seventies and busy as ever, **Luci Swindoll** helps us learn how to slow down and stop. **Suanne Camfield** accepts that being good enough really *is* good enough. When we're feeling stuck and restless and still want to make a difference in the world, **Jennifer Grant** shows us where to start.

Sometimes letting go is deadly serious. **Julie Owens** was physically abused by her husband—until she finally decided, *No more and never again.* Her essay empowers women toward self-worth and the courage needed to leave abusive relationships. And finally, eighty-four-year-old **Win Couchman** gives up cooking and her car keys, discovering that even the releases we think look like losses can actually be occasions for greater grace. As you read these women's stories, be prepared to let go of your fears, to turn toward a bountiful future.

Shelly Wildman

Shelly is the author of *First Ask Why: Raising Kids to Love God Through Intentional Discipleship*. She's married to her college sweetheart, Brian, and is mom to three amazing adult daughters. Shelly teaches writing at Wheaton College, where she earned a BA in literature. She also holds an MA in English education from the University of Illinois at Chicago. Shelly is a blogger, a monthly contributor to the *Mothers of Daughters* blog, and a speaker to women's groups in the Chicago area. You can follow Shelly at shellywildman.com.

Never Again—Period!

I was a late bloomer. Like all the other girls in fifth grade, I read the classic *Are You There, God? It's Me, Margaret* with a flashlight underneath the blankets in my bed. At school we giggled, maybe a little nervously, about the upcoming changes in our bodies. We cheered when, one by one, our friends got their periods.

But me? I waited.

The summer before eighth grade, I attended church camp and met a girl with an exotic-sounding name—something like Cindy or Samantha or Gina—who not only had gotten her period, but was already using (*gasp!*) tampons. My late-blooming brain could barely comprehend this; this girl was too sophisticated for me.

The blessed event finally took place for me much later, and it wasn't long before I thought, *Is this what all the fuss was about?* From that day on, I hated having my period.

Some of the reasons are obvious: it's messy, it's inconvenient, and at times it's painful (like the time in college when I spent two full days in bed with debilitating cramps).

And let's talk about the financial implications for a minute. The amount of money I've spent on feminine products in the approximately thirty-seven years that I've been having periods could fund a small country.

Add to that the fact that I have three daughters, and I've probably spent the equivalent of the GDP of Liechtenstein on pads and tampons alone. I know some women relish their periods as proof of their fertility, femininity, and fruitfulness. For me, it just meant *Ugh. Here we go again.*

I lean toward what the early twentieth-century author Florence King once said: "A woman must wait for her ovaries to die before she can get her rightful personality back. Post-menstrual is the same as premenstrual; I am once again what I was before the age of twelve: a female human being who knows that a month has thirty days, not twenty-five."[1]

Further research has proven that I'm not all that off-base in my feelings. When women in Europe were asked to cite the positive consequences of menopause, the number one answer given was *no. more. periods.* Most of us are glad to be able to say "Never again!" to that aspect of our lives.

But what about having babies? We all know that along with the "never again" of periods comes the "never again" of giving birth. Many women aren't quite so quick to cast aside that aspect of their womanhood. It's difficult, after all, to think of our bodies in a new way, to give up the life-giving aspects of our physical tent and succumb to *wearing* a tent. And yet, at some point it becomes an inevitable fact: our bodies are just not capable of producing life anymore. It's like craving Chick-fil-A on a Sunday—no matter how great the craving, it just isn't going to happen.

And so, to some extent, we grieve.

Whatever your feelings are about your monthly cycle, I'd venture to guess that we all would agree that hitting this stage of life—"the change" as the old ladies in my church called it with a blush and a giggle—takes its toll, both physically and emotionally. Whether we fall into the "elated" category or the "all torn up" camp, we've got some feelings.

Of course, there are the physical changes: hot flashes, night sweats, insomnia, irritability, moodiness (*who, me?*), headaches, joint pain, teariness, forgetfulness . . . Need I go on?

Some mornings I look in the mirror and wonder *Who are you?* I don't recognize this body anymore—the body I used to count on to be strong and, dare I say it, *thin?* These days, no matter how much I exercise or keep track of what I've eaten, my body just doesn't respond. It's become a stubborn child who refuses to be manipulated into compliance.

My emotions have failed me too. I used to be strong in this area as well, able to fight back tears, unaffected by the show of emotion of those around me. But no more. Give me a good coffee commercial—a soldier comes home from war, say, and surprises his parents by making a pot of coffee—and I'm a puddle on the floor. Don't even get me started on church where I pretty much cry every week. If "Great Is Thy Faithfulness" is on the docket, forget it—I'm a blubbering mess, and you can be sure that every person in my family will be furtively glancing down the row to see how soon the first tear leaks out.

But with all this doom-and-gloom about menopause symptoms— we've been warned *ad nauseam*—there is still hope. Researchers have found that even though physical and emotional symptoms are likely to occur, some more flagrant than others, "women's adjustment to menopause can be shaped by the social context in which this life transition occurs."[2] Research from the North American Menopause Society (who knew there was such a thing?) concurs: "The attitude with which you embark upon this transition can have a tremendous impact on your experience of it."[3] The NAMS website goes on to say that if we change some of our negative feelings about this stage of life, we might be able to reduce some of our symptoms. In other words, think positive thoughts and menopause will go more smoothly for you.

Now, I'm all for the power of positive thinking, but I wonder what, exactly, should or could that look like for a woman of faith? Some research into "Christian response to menopause" revealed interesting results. I found solutions like "pray more" or "husbands should show compassion to their wives" (I kind of liked that one) or, my favorite, "the Hallelujah diet." I guess holding up holy hands burns calories faster than walking.

I think as Christian women we can do better than that. Rather than thinking of menopause as something to dread, what if we just called it what it is: a change of life? (Maybe those women of a bygone era had the right idea after all.) It *is* a change. A new stage of life. Even though it may come with some complications and concerns, this new phase is also inevitable. As the writer of Ecclesiastes reminds us, "For everything there is a season." Even menopause. I wonder what would happen if we simply leaned into that season and accepted it for what it is.

But even as I write these words so flippantly, I have to admit—I hate change. I've always hated change. Change, for me, has either meant tragedy or hard work, neither of which I am inclined to relish. I've already mentioned my changing body, which leaves me feeling less than beautiful these days, and my changing emotions are, if I'm completely honest, a bit scary. I have a feeling that this new season of life will get harder and life-as-it-was will seem easy compared to the days ahead. I fear going into that dark, dark tunnel and not being able to find my way out.

The famous writer Joan Didion has suffered her entire life with migraine headaches and has learned, over time, to simply accept that they are a part of her life, even calling a migraine, "my friend." She writes that she no longer fights these attacks; rather, she says, "I lie down and let it happen." And when the attack is over, Didion has a new perspective on her life: "I open the windows and feel the air, eat gratefully, sleep well. I notice the particular nature of a flower in a glass on the stair landing. I count my blessings."[4]

Perhaps I, in my fear and discomfort about the changes my body is experiencing, should come to think of menopause as my friend. Yes, it ravages. Yes, it changes me. Yes, it takes me down dark and narrow alleys of forgetfulness and fatigue. But it is God's way of making me into the woman he created me to be, and it is a good and necessary change.

A late bloomer I may have been once, a long time ago, but I hope to change that now. In this season of life, while I'm happy to rid myself of excess expenses (bye-bye, Lichtenstein!) and the pain and discomfort of monthly periods, I hope I can also shed myself of something else: fear of the changes that still lie ahead. I hope to embrace my womanhood with all the courage I can muster and to be able to laugh, joyfully, as the woman in Proverbs does, at the time to come.

Notes

1. Florence King, *Lump It or Leave It* (New York: St. Martin's Press, 1990), 8.
2. Judy R. Strauss, "Contextual Influences on Women's Health Concerns and Attitudes Toward Menopause," *Health and Social Work* 36, no. 2 (May 2011): 122.

3. Leslee Kagan, "Make Your Menopause a Positive Experience," The North American Menopause Society, accessed January 25, 2018, https://www .menopause.org/for-women/menopauseflashes/menopause-symptoms -and-treatments/make-your-menopause-a-positive-experience.
4. Joan Didion, "In Bed," *The White Album: Essays* (1968; New York: Farrar, Straus and Giroux, 1990), 172.

Julie Owens

Julie has worked in the domestic violence field for almost thirty years. Her story is featured in the documentaries *Broken Vows: Religious Perspectives on Domestic Violence* and *When Love Hurts*. She has developed a church-based transitional shelter, counselor training programs, and trauma therapy research at the National Center for PTSD. She and her son found great peace when they visited her dying ex-husband in prison several years ago. She is now happily remarried. Her website is domesticviolenceexpert.org.

Leaving the Night Behind

My first inkling that something was terribly wrong was the evening of our wedding day. I was thirty-two, full of dreams and so in love with my new husband. Arriving at our honeymoon hotel, David suddenly exploded, "You've stayed here before, haven't you? Who were you with?" I was utterly taken aback. Had he slapped me in the face, the shock would have been no greater. When he saw my stunned look, he quickly stuttered an apology. I wanted to chalk it up to wedding day jitters, but an uncomfortable knowing settled in my spirit. The effervescent joy of my wedding day evaporated.

During our courtship, David had been easygoing, not showing the slightest hint of jealousy or disrespect. At our wedding, a friend had read my favorite Bible chapter, 1 Corinthians, "Love is patient and kind. Love is not jealous or boastful or proud or rude. It does not demand its own way" (13:4–5 NLT). As a teen, I had been taught to replace the word *love* with the name of a boy I liked. If the words still rang true, I was told, his actions would be based on love. I had never forgotten that. My pastor father and my mother had always been wonderfully respectful and affectionate. I immediately knew that David's behavior was neither normal nor godly.

Within weeks, the honeymoon was over. David's jealousy grew into routine accusations of infidelity and interrogations. When he exploded, he swore at me and called me horrible names. This was not the man I had fallen in love with! I remember thinking, "I married Dr. Jekyll but I woke up with Mr. Hyde." Out of the blue, he would escalate into a rage that ended in his ripping the phone out of the wall, throwing dishes of food, or pounding walls. Had I not become pregnant just two weeks after the wedding, I might have left David sooner. I was old enough to know I couldn't change another person. But I did believe my vows were sacred and I knew that God can and will change us if we ask.

Before I met David, I had been a joyful free spirit, traveling and exploring other cultures. I'd visited the Middle East, Asia, the Hawaiian Islands, and most of the states. I'd settled in an old barn-turned-cabin in rural Texas with a dear friend who had left her husband. Until hearing her experience, I never understood why a woman would stay with a man who beat her. But I knew them both well. She didn't fit my stereotype of a victim, and he didn't fit my idea of an abuser. I had so much to learn and no idea I would soon do so in the hardest way possible.

On good days, David and I enjoyed each other's company. On bad days, I hated being alone, isolated with him in the country. David would scream, block the door, or pin my arms and hide my keys and wallet. After just two months of marriage, I tearfully asked him, "Why didn't you ever treat me this way before the wedding?"

He looked me right in the eye and calmly replied, "Because you never would have married me." I was stunned. I'd been purposely betrayed!

After just two and a half months of marriage I was miserable. I confided in a few people, the pastor who married us, my OB/GYN, and a substance abuse counselor I knew. I was told to pray harder, to give it time, to de-stress, and to attend Codependents Anonymous (CODA) meetings. I went to a CODA group and shared about David's mistreatment of me. One man seemed annoyed and blurted out, "If he called you a chair, would it make you a chair?" Another advised, "Just see the word *sick* flashing on his forehead." When I left that meeting, I felt worse than ever.

After three months, I reached a breaking point. David was harassing me during the day and staying out at night. One night he calmly woke me with a loaded gun pointed at his heart.

"I'm going to kill myself, Julie," he said. "I know you're going to leave me."

Horrified, I pled, "Oh my god, David, give me that gun!" After promising I would not leave him, he finally relinquished it. I knew I could no longer stay. All night I planned my escape to my family in Hawaii.

I made it safely. Surrounded by supportive family and friends, life became peaceful again. While there, I met with counselors, pastors, and church leaders. At their urging, after three months I worked out a plan for a trial reconciliation. We reunited and I was cautiously hopeful. We shared a home with my parents and began joyfully preparing for our baby's arrival. We painted and decorated the nursery, attended marriage counseling, and attended my home church where Dad was the pastor. Despite our efforts to start over, though, David's old jealousy and behaviors reemerged. He insisted I carry a pager and call him immediately when paged. If I went out without him, he made me so miserable that it was easier to just stay home. Over the next months, he purposely drove erratically to frighten me. He harassed and deprived me of sleep. After the baby was born, he threatened to take Josh from me. Through all of this, in my mind I would sing Selah's "You Are My Hiding Place" over and over, committing myself to the strength of the Lord.

One Saturday night as I slept, David grabbed me and pressed a carpet knife blade into my wrist. He was enraged. "If you scream, I'll cut you!" Then the accusations again: "Who were you talking to on the phone? I kept calling and it was busy every time! Who was it?" He pressed me into the bed with all his weight. I was paralyzed with fear. All night he terrorized me, accusing me of being unfaithful. In between his accusations, he'd warn, "If you try to call the police or wake your father, I'll kill him!" Now I no longer feared just for myself, but for my whole family. I filed for divorce the next day and David reluctantly moved out.

Two weeks later, I returned to our darkened house one evening after dinner with Dad and church friends. When I opened the door, David ambushed me, beat me, and held a knife to my throat, saying, "I'm here to kill your father." When Dad came in, David attacked him with the knife. As we struggled, I was stabbed in the stomach. I cried out for help and I heard a voice, "Go turn on the light. When he sees what he's done, he'll run." I obeyed. When the light revealed our bloodied bodies, David ran. Suddenly it was over. We had survived. Our wounds were serious, but treatable. David was arrested and eventually sentenced to many years in prison.

In the days that followed, I found comfort and insight in Scriptures that seemed to speak directly to me. "The words of his mouth were smoother than butter, but war was in his heart: his words were softer than oil, yet were they drawn swords" (Psalm 55:21 KJV). "Everyone who does evil hates the light, and will not come into the light for fear that their deeds will be exposed" (John 3:20).

My journey to healing was a long process, not an event. The secular domestic violence programs that helped and educated me were an integral part of my recovery. My church's support was key. We formed a domestic violence committee and started a transitional shelter for battered women and children. I left special education to return to college and focus on domestic violence victim advocacy. It was not an easy road, but it has been a rewarding one.

Today I travel nationally and internationally, training professionals and faith leaders and testifying as an expert witness in court. Every year I meet hundreds of women over forty who are living in the hell of domestic violence. Most have been married for years, but many are in long-term dating relationships. Some are newlyweds. The majority are professionals, and invariably they are all friendly, intelligent, kind women who cannot understand how their lives have spun so terribly out of control. They have done everything they can think of to stop the abuse, to no avail. Most who are believers have been urged by pastors, Christian counselors, and church leaders to "pray and stay" and often even to "obey." They tell me, "I don't want my marriage to end. I just want the abuse to stop." I assure them they are not alone and tell them that God hates abuse and does not want them to suffer; that when a husband abuses his wife, he has broken the marriage covenant and she is free to divorce. I tell them they are not obligated to stay and suffer; they are free to pursue safety, justice, and peace.

Sometimes when death brushes near, we learn the hardest lessons of life, but we may also receive some of its greatest gifts. I have learned many "never agains" through my experiences. Never again will I take for granted that when someone says, "I love you" that they mean what I mean when I say those words. Never again will I judge another woman for the choices she makes when she is being abused. Never again will I assume that because a woman has not been hit, she is not a victim of domestic violence. Never again will I tolerate a man's disrespect or attempts to control me. Perhaps most importantly, though, never again will I doubt God, that in the darkest, most hopeless of life's circumstances, God will still lead me to the light.

Jeanne Murray Walker

Jeanne is the author of a memoir, *Geography of Memory: A Pilgrimage Through Alzheimer's*, and eight books of poetry, most recently *Helping the Morning*. Her poetry and essays have appeared in numerous journals, including *Poetry*, *Image*, *The Atlantic Monthly*, and *Best American Poetry*. She's received many fellowships as well as sixteen nominations for The Pushcart Prize. Jeanne serves as a mentor in the Seattle Pacific University MFA program and travels widely to give readings and run workshops. Visit jeannemurraywalker.com.

I Renounce Snap Judgments—Again

I was inching forward in a line at our local Rite Aid to pick up a prescription. Behind me stood a woman with unkempt wiry gray hair and sallow, saggy skin. She was dressed in a grayish cotton shirt and pants of the kind you might buy for two bucks at a down-on-its-luck thrift shop. The picture of what I hope I will not become someday.

"If I want Advil, they told me I have to see the pharmacist," she grumbled. She was dragging a canvas shopping bag behind her like a reluctant dog on a leash. "Maybe I'll just make some meth."

I laughed, imagining her cooking drugs on her stovetop. She laughed too: a small joke between us. I had presumed she was too unhip and ill-educated to know that a person can make meth from Advil. In retrospect, I realize she might be a professor at Bryn Mawr. I wish I could say I offered her my place in line, but I'm not yet that evolved in my practice of empathy.

What this episode revealed to me is how easily I can make snap judgments about people; they zero out compassion. Compassion, after all, is feeling *with* someone, experiencing the world through their eyes. I'd like to give up my tendency to make snap judgments, give it up for Lent and never take it back after Easter. I'd prefer to leave my heart open to surprises.

Giving up snap judgments is more complicated than it appears, because some of them are so helpful. By the time you're fifty, a lot of things have happened to you and you get good at *reading* the world. If you drive a car, for example, you have to guess what insane thing the drivers around you will do. Experience with driving helps you make those predictions. Without experience, when I was younger, I couldn't make accurate judgments.

When I was nineteen and deeply trusting and protected and wanted more than anything to see the world, I flew from our Chicago suburb to the Peruvian jungle for the summer. On the way back, I camped out for the night in a plastic chair in the Miami airport. I could not afford to stay in a hotel. I had three dollars in my pocket and a plane ticket home to Chicago after a flight from Lima, Peru, where I had spent the summer. I passed several hours talking to a man in a business suit—about Hemingway's novels, about civil rights marches, about the Vietnam War, which we both opposed. We had not been drinking. There was nothing sleazy or odd about our conversation. His plane was scheduled to go out in a couple of hours. He was flying home to his wife and children.

He asked whether I had ever seen the Atlantic Ocean, which I had not. He offered to rent a car and show it to me. I accepted, because I had spent my life in the Midwest and suddenly felt I could not bear to leave the East Coast without glimpsing the water. We drove to the shore through almost deserted streets as the sun was rising like a red lozenge in the eastern sky.

Now I am old enough to be the mother of that young woman and I want to yell to her: *Stop!*

It's possible that this businessman had planned our beach encounter from the very beginning, but I doubt it. I don't think from the get-go it was for him about sex. However, in the end, that was what it came down to. I escaped because I could talk. I talked him out of it.

That is to say, my judgment about him was not entirely wrong. He was decent enough to listen and to recognize how utterly I was without any experience of or desire for an encounter like that. He politely drove me back to the airport. I boarded my plane at seven that morning, traumatized but grateful. I added to my suitcase of belongings the knowledge that not all men who talked about civil rights and the war were as trustworthy as my male friends at college.

It's the same with tomatoes. Not everything at Acme labeled "tomato" tastes like the tomatoes our neighbor Carol gives us from her garden in the summer.

I don't intend to give up helpful judgments about things like tomatoes. I hope to get better at them, while renouncing my tendency to try people around me in the court of my mind, especially when it isn't even useful or necessary.

I was sitting in my Honda on a rosy, soft-spoken summer morning when a young woman driving a beat-up red truck pulled up at the stoplight next to me. So lurid was the death rock blasting from her open window two feet from me that her truck vibrated and my Honda quivered like a wounded animal. I felt outrage at the way she stomped on and overruled and crushed the summer. I rolled up my window, but the blare penetrated the glass as if it were plastic wrap. We sat at the red light for what seemed forever while her music went on murdering peace. She swayed to its vicious rhythm. I began to feel that she had driven there intentionally to blast her music at me. When she caught me looking at her, she tossed her black hair and stared back in a way that I interpreted as poisonous.

Then I realized that to her I looked old. (I don't have the faintest idea what I'm doing in a body that looks old. It's not my fault.) I imagined that she was a spoiled narcissist.

That's everything I know about the girl in the red truck—what I saw of her at the stoplight one day last summer. She might have been an honor student taking peonies to her dying mother. Even if she wasn't motivated by a good reason like that, it is still wrong for me to hate her. Hating is hard work. It's bad for a person's heart.

I am dismayed that as I get older I can feel myself making more snap judgments. I have googled enough to know that every blessed organ in the body gets more rigid as I age—the eyes, the heart, the kidneys, the brain. I know I am less adaptable than I used to be, even about small things.

On the other hand, there are some snap judgments I can barely bring myself to reverse, even in retrospect. This morning I almost hit a bicyclist. I was turning right. He sailed through a red light and wheeled in front of me. I jammed my foot onto the brake and skidded. A grocery bag on the front seat crashed to the floor. Cars honked. Without looking up, the kid glided between lanes of traffic and disappeared. My heart galloped; my hands sweated.

I could hear the crunch of metal and feel his bike splintering under my tires. In my mind's eye, I saw him arching through the air and thudding onto the road. He lay there, pulpy and bleeding, curled up on the pavement, looking like my own son.

All day this scene has been replaying itself in my body. It's getting dark now and I'm pretty sure I won't sleep tonight. Meanwhile, he is probably safe in his bedroom, blissfully texting his friends, unaware that he was almost killed. I am trying to figure out how to give up my own malice and ill will about this.

Jesus said his followers should become like children. Children who have been treated well tend to be curious and open, at least until they're about eleven. They haven't made five million decisions. They haven't formed calluses all over their judgment mechanisms the way we have.

Jesus didn't even live to be forty. Was that partly because he never made snap decisions about the people he met? For example, consider the tax collector, the guys who fished for a living, or the lady who had five husbands. He ran around with people who were not considered classy. In the courts of the day, those friends counted against him. One of them turned him in to the police. If I want to take him seriously, I need to remember: he warned us not to judge others because we never know the whole story and we are never impartial.

That is why I am taking a vow against making snap decisions, even though, at my age, I know what I'm up against. Soon I will again find myself holding someone I don't know responsible for what is not her fault. As the apostle Paul remarked, we are always doing what we don't want to do. It would be foolish for me to say "Never again."

Taking a vow against snap judgments is like building a wall at a beachfront house. Yes, maybe you can keep some water out of your yard, but you can't hold back the ocean—not any more than you will be able to entirely avoid verdicts that cancel out your empathy. At two a.m., when you hear the wind raging in the pines, whipping tons of water onto your front porch, you hunker under the sheets in despair. Tomorrow you will pull on your boots, wade out, assess, and try to repair the damage. You will dry out the porch furniture. You will apologize to the person you have misjudged, or maybe not; but you will feel the loss of a bond you might have enjoyed.

By then the ocean will appear as calm and obedient as a well-trained golden retriever.

You will try to believe once again that it's important to separate the ocean from the land. You will renew your vow not to make snap decisions and you will feel the sunlight, which momentarily falls around you like grace.

Shannon Ethridge

Shannon is a best-selling author, international speaker, certified life coach, and advocate for healthy sexuality with a master's degree in counseling/human relations from Liberty University. Shannon is the author of twenty-two books, including the best-selling Every Woman's Battle series, *The Sexually Confident Wife*, and *The Fantasy*. Shannon and her husband, Greg, have been married twenty-five years, have two amazing college-age children, and happily reside in an empty nest in Tyler, Texas. Learn more at shannonethridge.com.

Make No Mistake

If I had a dime for every time someone has mistaken me for fellow author and speaker Staci Eldredge, I'd be a very rich woman. I guess our names are so similar that it's easy for people to get confused. But sometimes it's not our *identity* people mistake. Sometimes they mistake our *purpose*.

I served on a particular ministry campus for almost ten years, teaching college-age women the joys of living a life of sexual and emotional integrity. But I'd also grown with my audience since my youth pastor days in the early nineties and often ministered to girls who'd grown up to become adult women who struggled not just with sexual integrity outside of marriage, but also with sexual intimacy *inside* of marriage. I began to see my purpose as being an advocate for healthy sexuality, regardless of one's season of life.

After completing the Every Woman's Battle series, I proposed another book to my publisher, *The Sexually Confident Wife*, where I planned to coach married women on how to let go of past baggage, low self-esteem, and negative body image and connect intimately with their husbands without guilt, shame, or inhibition. Random House loved the idea, and I loved researching and developing the manuscript over the next year, complete with professional artistic sketches of "real women"—including cellulite ripples, stretch marks, saggy boobs, flat chests, pregnant bellies, and all!

When *The Sexually Confident Wife* released, my publisher flew me to New York for a live interview with Kathy Lee Gifford and Hoda Kotb on *The Today Show*. I was flying high, feeling as if I was doing exactly what God had called me to do—*to boldly go where no Christian woman had ever gone before!*

Upon my return home, however, I experienced a record-screeching, bubble-bursting moment. One of the campus leaders saw the interview and invited me into his office where he kindly explained that it was time for our ministries to part ways. As long as *sexual integrity* was my platform, they were tickled pink. But when I made *sexual intimacy* part of that platform, they blushed, and I got a pink slip.

A few hours later, I was sitting on a plane bound for Michigan to visit a friend, noticing how the raindrops were cascading down my window at about the same rate as the tears were streaming down my cheeks. It was the first time I'd ever been fired from a ministry position (although they insisted that I wasn't being "fired"). I was shocked and bewildered . . . confused and angry . . . scared and scarred. *God . . . How? How could you let this happen?*

I thought of one of my life verses: "Unless a kernel of wheat falls to the ground and dies, it remains only a single seed. But if it dies, it produces many seeds" (John 12:24). I realized that even if my dream job was dead, God was still in the resurrection business. God promises to give us the desires of our heart when we delight ourselves in him. I pondered what I wanted my life to be about and what kind of legacy I wanted to leave behind. Four things came to mind:

I wanted to encourage women to live with sexual integrity.
I wanted to teach couples to embrace a lifestyle of healthy sexual intimacy.
I wanted to inspire others to enjoy an intimate relationship with Jesus Christ.
I wanted to coach people who felt called to build their own ministry.

I was already working diligently toward the first three goals, and no longer being affiliated with the ministry wouldn't hinder those at all. I would continue teaching *Women at the Well* classes and would continue personal coaching, not just with college-age girls, but with both single and married adults. The horizon was already looking much clearer and brighter.

The last goal—coaching people toward building their own ministry—had been germinating for some time. As the *Every Man's Battle* and *Every Woman's Battle* movement had spread over the previous five plus years, I was often asked, "How can I learn to do what you do? How does one get a book published? How do I become a speaker?"

I truly wanted to cheer them on but couldn't imagine how I could possibly find time to become *their* cheerleader when I was so busy managing my own ministry.

But at the ripe old age of forty, I suddenly had time—more time than ever before with my shiny new pink slip in hand. I contemplated how I *could* actually do more to help others find their own voice and discover their own people-helping passions beyond just offering a prayer and a pat on the back. I considered that maybe God had allowed me to experience such success in my thirties simply so I'd have plenty of time in my forties and beyond to inspire others to make their own ministry dreams come true.

Suddenly, with this new fire burning in my belly, I was actually *excited* that I'd been fired! I actually *thanked* God for all that had happened in the past twenty-four hours. I was overjoyed at the freedom I had to take this idea and run with it. The vision didn't have to fit into another ministry's mold or fit neatly under their umbrella. It was *my* vision . . . *my* baby . . . *my* opportunity . . . *my* responsibility! God had conceived this in my spirit, and I knew it would be both a blessing and a burden to push through the pain required to give birth to it.

Soon, amid the joyful tears, the letters B-L-A-S-T came to mind. I mentally played with them, realizing they could be an acronym for "Building Leaders, Authors, Speakers, and Teachers"—which was exactly what I felt called to do!

I saw myself and a friend standing in front of a vacant lot with a video camera rolling, explaining month by month what was taking place as something incredibly substantial was being built. I grabbed my journal and began jotting down ideas about how to build a ministry from the ground up. Over the next year, B.L.A.S.T. evolved into a twelve-month online mentorship program allowing anyone in the world with a passion for people and an internet connection to be guided and inspired to bring to life whatever dream God had planted in them. It's been one of the most fruitful and rewarding endeavors of my life to watch these various ministries and businesses sprout and blossom—like watching beloved children give birth to many grandchildren!

I'd never thought of myself as being a grandmother in my forties (my children were barely out of their teens). But I've gladly embraced the role of a *spiritual* grandmother. The world needs more of them.

If you need to let go of something good to make room for something better, let this chapter be your pink slip. Make no mistake about your own identity *or* your purpose. You are God's creation, girlfriend—put on the planet at this particular time for a particular purpose. And don't let any perceived "failure" hinder that identity or purpose. Failures are often God-orchestrated opportunities to sharpen your spiritual focus and to prune your life so that you can be far more fruitful in the long run!

Amy F. Davis Abdallah

Dr. Amy lives just outside New York City. She writes, speaks, and teaches to empower women and men to live out their true selves, fostering transformation through rites of passage and her recent book, *The Book of Womanhood*. Amy is a professor who teaches at home and abroad and a mentor who goes deep with her mentees. In her free time, she enjoys exercise, photography, climbing mountains, adventuring with her husband and sons, and learning languages. Find her on the web at amyfdavisabdallah.com and on twitter @amyfdavisa.

The Fetters and Freedom of Family

I'm forty-three and I'm exhausted. I collapse into my sliding rocker to nurse four-month-old Nathan and to scroll through my Facebook feed on my phone. Ah, there's my friend Hannah in Vail skiing with her husband, all bundled up with big smiles and a rugged snowy mountain view. I'm not too envious because I hate the cold, but last summer Hannah traipsed through the green fields and cobblestoned streets of Ireland. I followed her Facebook posts from my bed with pregnancy-swollen ankles, after a long day chasing Joseph, my two-year-old, in the hot sun. Hannah is just a few years older, but she's free to wander the world with gusto while I am tied to potty-training mishaps, diapers, and my newfound homebody life.

As I scan the last of the snowy grins, Nathan pulls loudly off my breast and the phone crashes to the floor. I hold my breath and hope the noise doesn't waken Joseph, who's napping in the next room. Joseph's fever, cough, and constantly running nose have kept us up for the past week. I've contemplated quitting this gig more than once.

I wearily pick up my phone and give Nathan my other side. Moments later, Joseph's cries begin as a whimper but quickly become a full-fledged wail. I stand awkwardly without detaching Nathan and head in to comfort my sick boy. Thank God no one has taken pictures of my less-than-graceful attempts to keep Nathan latched.

I never imagined my life this way. I was supposed to have a college sweetheart-turned-husband and bear four kids in my twenties, a young, energetic mom. After they grew, I'd head back to work and join Hannah on various international trips.

Long singleness gave me the freedom to teach elementary school in Asuncion, Paraguay. Later, I returned stateside to pursue seminary and a PhD in liturgical studies. I worked eight years as a Nyack College professor before I even met the man who would become my husband.

Hannah and I were traveling together, touring early Christian sites in the Middle East, when I met him. She was about to be empty nested and was traveling with me, the single and free one. She watched as we began our relationship-now-turned-family.

I never imagined marrying older and having my first child after turning forty-one. When I first held Joseph—wriggling wet in his still-attached body—I immediately noticed his mile-long eyelashes. At two and half, when I check on him at night, they lie peacefully on his bright cheeks as he sleeps.

At four months, Nathan's the happiest baby I've ever seen, with the biggest and most gurgly grin intended for me, his mama. Even in the wee hours, when he awakens to flail his arms and legs out of the swaddle, he sports a wide toothless smile that seems to say, "Hi there, world!" I groggily respond, grateful that he's not crying loudly, and wish for more sleep.

Before my kids were born, I taught evenings and worked from a quiet and reflective home. Now, I'm a strange hybrid of full-time professor of theology and Bible blended together with being a stay-at-home mom. I still seek to read, write, and create lessons but often work in an atmosphere that's utter pandemonium. It's hard to find time to just get coffee or a haircut while I juggle my world.

These days, Hannah is posting every wonderful and exotic place she visits, while I'm hoping there's no dried spit-up on me when I finally get to the office. Her world is expanding, while mine is closing in. Her life and pictures are public, but even my photos are private now. They feel too sacred to share with the world.

The day Joseph is finally well again, I carry his red Radio Flyer tricycle and plunk it down on the trail. Joseph sits on it, holds the handle-bars, and immediately starts pushing the ground with his feet. He's clad in his gray wool toggle coat and blue monkey pajama bottoms. He lifts both feet at the same time, rapidly brings them down, and forges ahead like a rocket. He squeals with delight.

I quickly catch up and place his sneakered feet on the pedals, saying, "Push this foot, push this other foot . . ." His feet go around until the right one reaches the apex and abruptly falls off. I squat and replace it, repeat my "push this foot" mantra, and half stand again. His feet fall, I repeat some more, and then I start to feel it in my lower back. I give up, sit back from the squat, knees up, hands behind to support me as I watch him.

Joseph gets off the trike and turns around to sit in a backwards strad-dle, gray wool hood blown off to reveal his wild uncut hair, grin reveal-ing the fun. Finally, he walks away, holding the handlebars with his right hand, catching the air with his left. From my spot on the ground, I've snapped some photos. I will send them to his godmother.

I think about Hannah and realize that when we traveled, she had her family on her mind and heart. She didn't travel as independently as I did back then, single and free. She called home, checked in, and took care. Each season of parenting is demanding.

I said goodbye to independence in order to say hello to family. As Thomas Aquinas said, "Every choice is a renunciation." I no longer live alone and life will never again be just about me. I ponder the freedom that I will never again experience. Even though it was an independence I sometimes hated in my longing for a family, it was sweet and helped make me who I am. If I'm honest, sometimes I miss it.

I am reminded of the saying, "The greatest act of freedom is to choose to be bound." I choose these family fetters every day. I want to live this life—this family life, the one I never imagined—with gusto, enjoying those who depend on me as I cherish, photograph, and ponder each sacred experience.

Andrea Stephens

Andrea is a former model who served as beauty editor for Focus on the Family's *Brio* magazine. She has authored sixteen books for teen girls and founded The B.A.B.E. Event, which teaches women of all ages that *in Christ* they are beautiful, accepted, blessed, and eternally significant—a *real* B.A.B.E.! Andrea's thirty-year marriage ended abruptly, forcing her to carve out a new life, hand in hand with Jesus. She is pursuing her master's degree in practical theology and enjoys oil painting, a round of golf, and long walks on the beach.

No More Comparing

I received the call from the fertility clinic at 6:27 a.m. that Sunday morning. "We're sorry, Mrs. Stephens, but there are no embryos to transfer today; in fact, two of the three eggs in the Petri dish did nothing at all. With the third, it appears that a sperm did penetrate the outer wall of the egg but that was it. There was no fertilization, no division." The in vitro fertilization had failed—again. Her voice faded out as my mind attempted to shift into survival mode. *You are fine. You are fine. You are fine. Get dressed, go to church, you are fine!* My mind was hearing the words out of my mouth, but my heart wasn't buying it. I was not fine. I was crushed and broken.

Thoughts and emotions were tumbling and colliding. Forget church. I just couldn't stand to see Tara's baby bump or watch the Olsons showing off their new twins. I just needed to get away, to be alone. I got in my car to make the hour drive to the beach where I could talk and walk with God. I cried most of the way there, asking God yet another round of "why" questions. I was primed for a big talk with him once that ocean air was swirling around me. But the talk turned into a one-sided shouting match because the first thing I saw as I walked in the sand were big mommy footprints next to little kid footprints. *Are you kidding me, Lord? Why did I have to see this right here, right now? Could I just get a break?*

My escape to the beach ended up being one more reminder that I was childless. I already had plenty of things bringing my babyless life to my attention, including my childhood rocking chair still awaiting use by my little ones.

It was all getting to be too much. Years of doctor appointments, invasive vaginal ultrasounds, fertility drug injections, blood draws, ovulation kits, hormone treatments, surgeries to remove painful cysts, and financial fallout. The spontaneous fun of sex had been replaced with timed relations or speeding to the clinic with my husband's sperm in a plastic sanitized cup to get washed, spun, and launched into my uterus. Plus, every time I started my period it felt like another brick piled onto my heart. It was wearing me down. The hand-knit baby booties on my dresser, intended to be a symbol of hope, were becoming a source of discouragement.

I had become an expert at politely declining baby shower invitations while sending nonemotional gifts like diapers and knowing how to redirect the conversation when I was asked for the zillionth time when we were going to start our own little family. I made continual effort to put on a happy face, but my relationships with longtime girlfriends and several women at the church were being strained as I isolated myself in an effort to hide the jealousy, envy, and grief that filled me.

Pulling away seemed easier than making all of us uncomfortable. I wanted them to be free to talk about their pregnancy or their kids, but my presence made it awkward for each of us. They didn't want to hurt my feelings. I didn't want the reminder that I didn't have a daughter to snuggle or a son to take bike riding. I imagine the attitude in my heart was showing all over my face. The continual question of *Why her and not me?* was growing into an obsession.

Yet, really, why her? My neighbor already had seven kids when she came over to tell me she was pregnant again. Really? The celebrity plastered all over the tabloids bragging about her successful IVF—the twins that were on their way! Really? The announcement that one of our ministry volunteers, who had two abortions during her wild years, was expecting. Really?

My jealous attitude of *Why her and not me?* was planting little seeds of bitterness and resentment—seeds that I knew would grow into ugly, uncontrollable bushy weeds if I didn't deal with them. But I didn't know how. What would be the thing that turned this all around? One afternoon after a good cry over my girlfriend's New Year's Eve pregnancy announcement, I whispered a reluctant, "Help me," to Jesus. He wasted no time.

The fact that she is having a baby has nothing to do with you!

Wait, what?

He repeated himself. Little by little the implications of that statement unfolded. Quite bluntly, I was being told that what God was doing in someone else's life was none of my business. It was his business.

It reminded me of the little conversation in John 21:15–22 between Jesus and Peter after the resurrection. Jesus was giving Peter his marching orders, so to speak. But Peter wanted to know what the plan was for John. Basically, Jesus put him in his place, saying, "What's that to you? You—follow me."

I began to see that comparing myself to other women was robbing me of entering into their pregnancy joy. It was eating away any chance for inner contentment. It kept me focused on what I did not have instead of what I did have. The growing jealousy kept me from fully recognizing and embracing what God *was* doing in my life. And to be honest, it was creating disappointment with the Lord for not giving me what I wanted. After all, we were good people, we were serving him in ministry, we would be great parents, and we had invested so much money, time, energy, hope, prayer, and applied all the faith we had. But still, nothing but failure.

I needed a change of focus. I needed to retrain my brain, trusting that my heart would fall in line. It started on a rainy afternoon with a latte and a blank notepad. My goal was to jot down everything I was aware of that the Lord had done and was doing in my life.

What could have been a tedious, painful task ended up being a reality check and a blessing. The pages began to fill with memories of the girls who received college funds through the scholarship pageant I directed and the breakfast Bible studies at our house where we were making disciples (and eating chocolate-chip pancakes) around the kitchen table.

There was the satisfaction of praying with girls at summer camp. Plus, my love for Jesus, teen girls, beauty, and fashion all coming together with my first book contract was truly a God thing.

I was offered my own column in *Brio* magazine and began to get invitations to speak at retreats, camps, and conferences. That led to the creation of The B.A.B.E. Event, where I taught (and still do) young women they are beautiful in God's sight, accepted by him, blessed with gifts and talents, and have an eternally significant purpose in life. Over the years, hundreds of girls received Jesus into their hearts at B.A.B.E.! In addition, I had the freedom to co-lead mission trips or sneak away for a night or two with my husband. God had indeed been at work all around me. He had been using me in ways that were unique to me. God is good like that—designing and creating each of us for the purpose he has planned.

Yes, I may not know the emotional bonding that can happen between a couple when their children are born. I may not hear anyone call me Mommy or give me sloppy wet kisses. But that was okay. A peace was growing inside of me where there used to be struggle. When I said goodbye to comparing my life with that of others and stopped longing for what they had that I didn't, things changed. God could work in this heart that was now looking to him and not around at everything else. God did not choose to change my situation but he changed my perspective, which changed everything.

Today I have friends of all ages. Some are just getting married, some are signing up for birthing classes, some are preparing to be grandmothers, while others are coaching their daughters' soccer teams, attending school plays, and planning graduation parties. And me? I am a fifty-something childless woman who never wants to compare herself with others to the point that it robs her of contentment, joy, and seeing how God is using her. I have learned to be grateful. That is an attitude that allows me to genuinely celebrate life with others and glorify my heavenly Father no matter what.

Michelle Van Loon

Michelle is the author of several books, including *Born to Wander: Recovering Our Pilgrim Identity.* She is cofounder of theperennialgen.com for midlife women and men and a contributor to a number of other sites as well. Learn more about her work at michellevanloon.com.

The Gift of Regret

I officially entered midlife in a fast-food restaurant at the height of the lunchtime rush. It couldn't have come at a worse time. One moment, I was eating an order of french fries; the next, without warning, I began to sob. It was not a dignified, gentle Jane Austen–heroine mist that could be staunched with a clean lace hankie, but a full-on blubber.

My three preteen kids sitting across the table from me could do nothing but inhale the rest of their burgers in awkward silence while simultaneously hoping that the ground would open up and swallow them alive so they wouldn't have to die of embarrassment. The one saving grace of this moment was that the kids thought my tears were a result of a traumatic event that had happened in our living room a couple of hours earlier.

I didn't have words to explain to them that the painful episode in question had almost instantly drained a decade-old well of sorrow buried inside of me, exposing a deep regret-polished boulder. I couldn't ignore my regret any longer, nor could I rebury it. It was too big. My ugly cry in the restaurant was both a plea for a do-over in life and the dawning of my realization that there is no such thing.

Regret serves a training purpose in our lives. One of the first things a newborn discovers is that her cry creates a response from the world: warm milk, comforting arms, a dry diaper. This cause and effect teaches the baby how the world works. It doesn't take long before a child graduates to some version of the old "the dog ate my homework" dodge to avoid uncomfortable short-term consequences.

As we move toward adulthood, we're wired for idealism—dreaming big dreams, making big plans. The passion that fuels idealism also fuels the way in which we make decisions. Impulsiveness and a lack of experience with weighing long-term consequences mean we make decisions that may leave us with a collection of mismatched, unprocessed regrets. Because we're very busy during those builder years of young adulthood—on the way to building relationships, families, and careers—we may not have the space to reflect on the consequences of those choices. But in those painful moments, hours before the fast-food oil hit my french fries, I learned that our loving God created that space in life for us. It's called midlife.

There's no way to get from the first half of life to the second except by moving through the crossroads of transition. In his book *Managing Transitions: Making the Most of Change,* author William Bridges describes transition as a three-part process. The first part is an ending that forces people to let go of some piece of their identity and the ways in which they engaged the world. He dubs the second phase "the neutral zone," that in-between, foggy portal between what was and what is to come. Bridges notes the neutral zone is when essential realignments occur. The third phase of transition is a new beginning, when people experience a new sense of purpose as a result of integrating the change that's occurred in their lives. The midlife transition is the neutral zone.

I'd experienced a definite end of one phase of my life a couple of hours before my midday meltdown when I had placed our first foster baby into the long-waiting arms of her adoptive mother. I expected I'd experience some grief as I said goodbye to the baby who'd spent the first weeks of her life with our family. I didn't expect that hard, sweet goodbye would usher me into the disorienting world of phase two.

Rhiannon's departure was a trigger, to be sure. But my deep grief overflowed as I looked at my three kids and realized how very quickly our time together was passing. Perhaps a perceptive counselor would have suggested to me that deciding to foster newborns was my way of trying to hold on to the past. I would have gone the counselor one better. I would have told him or her that I wasn't trying to recapture my past. I was trying to rewrite it in order to erase one of my deepest regrets.

When Jesus promised his followers abundant life—"I have come that they may have life, and have it to the full" (John 10:10)—he didn't add a regret clause, "except in cases where the party of the second part has stumbled, struggled, or sinned."

It didn't much matter. Years earlier, I'd penciled in the clause myself. The seeds of my sorrow were planted almost ten years earlier. July 25, 1986—a red-letter day, the day my youngest child was born. It should have been one of the most joyful days of my life.

It was, and it was one of the saddest too. My husband, Bill, and I had decided during that pregnancy that three children were enough. Enough, as in, "I really couldn't handle another slice of that triple-chocolate cheesecake. I'm stuffed." We were about to have our third baby in as many years, and we were stuffed. More accurately, we were depleted by the daily marathon of life with three children three and under. We decided I'd have a tubal ligation after the baby arrived.

We'd avoided the topic of our decision in our prayers to God. We never asked him his opinion about our family size. Instead, we told each other we just couldn't handle any more. Three kids were enough.

After Jacob was born, I was wheeled into surgery, still high on the ecstasy of a healthy birth and meeting our beautiful, peaceful little boy. As the surgical team was doing their prep work, my obstetrician—the man who'd delivered my baby just a couple of hours earlier—stopped and looked intently at me.

"You know, you don't have to do this," he said. "Are you sure you're ready to go ahead with the procedure?"

I've always wondered what prompted him to ask that question. Maybe he asked it of all of his young patients. I was only twenty-seven years old at the time. My mind raced: What would Bill say if I backed out now? How would we handle whatever it was that was coming next? The babies seemed to be coming fast and furious in our household, and our other attempts to slow the flow had not been successful.

I had the distinct sense that obeying God in that moment meant telling the doctor not to go ahead with the tubal ligation. Not that day. Probably not ever. But instead of hitting the pause button, I reverted to my default setting. I did what seemed right in my own eyes.

As the babies grew into toddlers, then preschoolers, regret started to nibble at the edges of my busy days. When I confessed those nascent regrets to my husband, he confessed that he'd had a few guilt pangs of his own about our decision. (A note here: Our individual convictions on this subject are not prescriptions for the decisions of others.) Our regret had much to do with making a long-term, permanent decision about our family based on our changeable emotions at the time instead of prayerful deliberation.

We learned that the tubal had left me with female plumbing problems. I scarred inside after the procedure. If I hadn't committed an unpardonable sin, I had certainly managed to indulge in an irreversible one.

My unresolved guilt festered for nearly a decade. When we began attending a church populated by a number of adoptive and foster families, I wondered if God had hit the family reset button for us. The finances required for adoption were daunting, to say the least, but we thought we could try foster parenting and see where it took us. Our kids were excited at the prospect of having a little baby come to live with us for a while. The social worker who evaluated our family and home prior to granting us a foster license told us we were a perfect family for the task.

She knew this was going to be a part of our family's ministry but had no idea that foster care was both penance and prayer for me. My unvoiced hope was that maybe one of the foster babies would be left with us—things like that happened once in a while, I knew—and it would be a sign that God really had forgiven me, and that I was worthy to mother another child in spite of my decision to have a tubal ligation a decade earlier.

My grief in the restaurant the day Rhiannon left us was sadness at letting her go, but also a revelatory moment when I began to come to terms with the fact that I could not go back to fix the past. I wanted more than anything to be able to right my wrong and turn my "if only" into a do-over.

The unforgiving nature of regret is best captured in Mary Shelley's words. The author of *Frankenstein* once observed that regret causes us to become "cannibals of our own hearts." Unresolved regret is a leech that steals from our present in order to feed the pain of our past, hindering our future in the process.

That fresh sorrow marked a reality; I'd finally begun to surrender to God by allowing remorse to begin its work in me. *The Message* paraphrase of 2 Corinthians 7:10 explains the work of this kind of godly sorrow: "Distress that drives us to God does that. It turns us around. It gets us back in the way of salvation. We never regret that kind of pain. But those who let distress drive them away from God are full of regrets, end up on a deathbed of regrets."

I now recognize that my breakdown in the noisy restaurant was an end of my first adulthood. As I groped after Jesus through the twilight of the neutral zone, it was the birth of my second adulthood, a gift at midlife from the One who was waiting to redeem my regrets for my good and his glory.

Luci Swindoll

Luci is an author, popular speaker, photographer, musician, artist, and world traveler who loves to share her joy of life with everyone she encounters. After thirty years with Mobil Oil and twenty years devoted to speaking and writing more than fifteen books, including *Simple Secrets to a Happy Life, Doing Life Differently*, and *I Married Adventure*, Luci says, "We don't need more tips for 'having it all,' but we could all use insight on 'having what matters.'"

Learn When to Stop

Knowing when to stop is one of the hardest exercises in the world. I'm seventy-three and still trying to learn it. And I mean stopping for any reason. Not just knowing when to retire—which seems logical in the fulfillment of a long working career—but knowing when to stop driving a car, stop traveling abroad, stop packing to move, stop trimming trees, or stop volunteering at church. I can name any number of things we do in our everyday lives that may have a stopping point, but when is that? The answer differs with each person.

Nobody can dictate when you have to stop doing something. Sometimes God puts on the brakes with health problems or other life circumstances, but apart from those, we rarely know the best time to stop doing something. How can we know for sure where the stopping point is in any activity? When is the best time to say no? What is the right moment to transition from one thing to another?

There is no definitive answer to these questions—and don't let anybody tell you there is. What might work for me might not work for you. And since I've tried twice to retire and it hasn't stuck, I'm not a good one to advise others on a proper stopping point. My father worked every day until well into his eighties, and that was long after retiring from his "last" job. I wrote my first book at fifty, traveled all over the world at sixty, and built my first house at seventy, so what will I be doing at eighty? Who knows? But unless I'm forced to, I have no intention of stopping.

Sometimes I feel like my life has just started because finally, *finally* I've learned how to truly live—how to enjoy a life that's balanced and fulfilled. I've figured out a few things that help me cope with the demands and vicissitudes of daily living. No one ever arrives, of course, but I'm a lot further along than I once was. I only wish I had known a long time ago about what I'm writing in this chapter. I wish someone had told a much younger me the best way to grow old, but they didn't. Maybe they didn't know either. Perhaps we learn the secret of aging by living fully right up to the edge of dying.

I read about women like Julia Child, who was ninety-two when she died. Until the very end of her life, she contributed to the culinary world more than any other person her age. She also taught us to savor life to the fullest. She once said, "A passionate interest in what you do is the secret of enjoying life, perhaps the secret of long life, whether it is helping old people or children or making cheese or growing earthworms."

May Sarton wrote in her journal, *At Seventy*, "I am a far more complete and richer person than I was at twenty-five, when ambition and personal conflicts were paramount and there was a surface of sophistication that was not true of the person inside." Or Grandma Moses—she lived one hundred one years—who at age one hundred, gave a birthday party for herself and danced a jig.

One of my friends at Women of Faith has an eighty-one-year-old grandmother who got a marriage proposal from her ninety-one-year-old "boyfriend." She can't decide whether or not to marry him . . . she wants to think about it. In the meantime, my friend suggested she hurry up before she's too old to be a flower girl. Don't you just *love* that?

In the mid-1990s, I read a delightful book called *Having Our Say: The Delany Sisters' First 100 Years*. It was by two black sisters, Sarah, one hundred three, and Bessie, one hundred one. When Bessie was growing up, she always said she'd like to be as old as Moses (who lived to be one hundred twenty), and she almost made it. When her sister said that, Sarah told her she herself would have to live to be one hundred twenty-two, so she could take care of her in her old age. They both claim they never thought anybody would be interested in hearing what "two old Negro women" had to say about life. But we're very interested in what they have to say, because life was always full of surprises to them and they made the most of every day. That's what we all want. We want to grow old like that. Who says we can't?

King David asked of the Lord in Psalm 90, "We live for seventy years or so (with luck we might make it to eighty), and what do we have to show for it? Trouble. Toil and trouble and a marker in the graveyard. . . . Oh! Teach us to live well! Teach us to live wisely and well!" (vv. 10, 12 MSG).

When I was in college, I had an elderly friend whom I loved dearly. Her name was Edna, and she was an unforgettable example of one who lived wisely and well. I was twenty, and she was eighty—a sixty-year age difference between us. But I never felt that difference when we were together—we were *girlfriends*. Edna's little home was a couple of blocks from the campus, and many Sundays I went with her daughter to visit Edna. Those were my favorite Sundays: church, lunch, Edna . . . in that order. She was the youngest old person I've ever known!

She loved opera and classical music, which rang out all over the house and into her yard, filled with hundreds of flowers in neat little beds running alongside a trimmed, manicured lawn. As the music played, she often sang along . . . a bit off-key, but who cared? She loved it, and everybody who stepped on that lawn did too.

Edna's house was crammed with books, in every corner—on the floor, the bed, the counter, the chairs. I'd talk with her about the ones she especially liked, and every now and then she'd break into poetry, quoting verse after verse. She read her books over and over and often said about a certain volume, "That one is as old as I am. I've read it four times."

Edna never stopped learning and growing. She memorized the Psalms while she washed dishes. She painted her own bathroom and made her own curtains. She shopped and cooked and cleaned and gardened. I'm sure she got tired and often needed help, but she never quit living or sharing her life with others. And she never complained.

The other day when I was roaming around in my own library, putting away books I'd been reading, I thought about Edna, wishing she could come over for tea. In part, because I wanted to show her my library and share my home with her, but mostly because I wanted to thank her for the legacy she passed on to me and never knew it. She's one of my sweetest memories of college days.

Scripture teaches us to number our days and to apply our hearts unto wisdom. It also says even though we're "wasting away" on the outside, we are being renewed inwardly day by day. Those two verses say a lot about the aging process. It's a lifelong journey that has neither a clear beginning nor clear ending. But there are signs along the way that one's body is changing. We see our hair turning gray. Wrinkles show up in our faces as they become seasoned and worn with time. We do things more slowly and deliberately. Our skeletal frame and skin seem to be lower to the ground, and what isn't lower or in need of repair has already fallen off! These are the signs of the outside wasting away.

But it's the inside that's being renewed daily. And *that's* what we want to concentrate on. It's those things inside we must learn to stop for. This is the secret of happy aging. Although obvious signs of physical changes are known to all of us, life's journey takes us beyond the obvious. It reaches inside and teaches us lessons we can only learn with our mind, spirit, and heart. The outward appearance becomes secondary to a far more endearing beauty and strength. The physical appearance of youth may be gone, but the capacity to love, experience, enjoy, share, and create grow even stronger.

Margot Starbuck

Margot is the author of five books, including *Unsqueezed: Springing Free from Skinny Jeans, Nose Jobs, Highlights and Stilettos*. Margot is a graduate of Westmont College and Princeton Theological Seminary. Margot enjoys speaking to audiences around the country about body image, adoption, neighbor-love, and the good news of God's presence with us and for us in the person of Jesus. Margot and her three teens live in Durham, North Carolina, in a community built around friends with disabilities. Learn more at margotstarbuck.com.

Skin Blotches and Jiggly Thighs

Gigi's ominous words still ring in my ears, "The sun is our enemy." Throughout my childhood, my grandmother would harangue my mother and her sister about the damaging effects of the sun's rays. Every summer at Lake Wawasee, Gigi would thrust upon her blond bikini-clad adult daughters sun visors and cover-ups to protect their skin. She'd maneuver sun umbrellas to shade them. She'd push zinc oxide in the vain hope that they'd slather it over their entire bodies. And like any sassy adult daughters, they ridiculed her every effort, oiling themselves and then baking to shiny dark perfection.

Today, at seventy-four, my mom, covered with blotches and patches and growths and melanomas, spends more time than she'd prefer with her dermatologist. She also wears long sleeves and long pants 365 days a year. And while I've only gotten one quick peek at the condition of my mom's legs, when she lifted her pant leg to show me some of the worst lesions, it's an image I won't soon forget. In fact, in my most desperate parenting moments, I will still threaten my teenage children, "If you don't obey me I'll make you look at Grandmommy's legs!" Though they have no idea what I'm talking about, they can discern enough from my tone to shape up their acts.

As a result of the enduring effects from tanning for sport, my mom has vowed to never again wear a bathing suit.

Never again.

～

For my mom, it's the scaly, blotchy skin that keeps her from pulling on an age-appropriate skirted one-piece. Some women will swear off bathing suits because the previously proud parts are now sagging. Still others, ashamed of once-firm thighs that now jiggle in the wind, will also choose to remain covered.

At forty-five, I've not yet been sidelined, like my mom, because I'm still waiting for the effects of years of sun damage to be fully revealed on my frame. Nor am I kept locked away due to gravity's ill effects. (Frankly, my proud parts were never really that proud anyway.) But I do jiggle. Oh, how I jiggle. Many self-respecting women in my shape would have hung up the lycra years ago. And yet, come sun damage or unwieldy gravity or jiggly thighs, I will never . . . ever . . . swear off swimming.

I like to make issues like scaly skin, sagging breasts, and jiggly thighs theological. What's the divine logic? Specifically, I'm dying to get a handle on the divine logic behind the aging situation. What holy madness drives wrinkles and age spots? (Besides, of course, the wily schemes of the enemy.) I've toyed with one weird possibility: Could this process that is clearly happening against our wills—as the volume of beauty products that promise to reverse aging's ill effects attests—be what Jesus has all along been inviting us to embrace with our wills?

"Hold on, Margot. Jesus never said anything about damaged skin, crows'-feet, Jell-O thighs, or declining breast altitude."

No, not in so many words. But to those who want to gain their lives—and maybe the attention of others—Jesus instructs us to lose our lives. Those who want to be first—say, in the Ms. Senior America pageant—should aim for last place. Those who want to increase—possibly in attractiveness—should decrease. Jesus even taught his friends that those who want to attract God's good favor should give themselves in ways that don't attract the good favor of others. Downward social mobility is exactly what Jesus has been inviting us to embrace all along. Though the apostle Paul wasn't thinking about decreasing muscle tone or loose scaly skin, he confirms, "We who are alive are always being given over to death for Jesus' sake, so that his life may also be revealed in our mortal body" (2 Corinthians 4:11).

In the radical economy of the kingdom, Jesus's life lived through our mortal bodies is exponentially more important than the opinion others hold of our mortal bodies!

In *Mere Christianity*, C. S. Lewis describes the type of person who lives into this freedom:

> Do not imagine that if you meet a really humble man he will be what most people call "humble" nowadays: he will not be a sort of greasy, smarmy person, who is always telling you that, of course, he is nobody. Probably all you will think about him is that he seemed a cheerful, intelligent chap who took a real interest in what *you* said to *him*. If you do dislike him it will be because you feel a little envious of anyone who seems to enjoy life so easily. He will not be thinking about humility: he will not be thinking about himself at all.[1]

Genius, right? This man, this woman, is the one who's been set free from chronic self-obsession.

Inspired by Lewis, in *The Freedom of Self-Forgetfulness*, Tim Keller notes, "The essence of gospel-humility is not thinking more of myself or thinking less of myself, it is thinking of myself less."[2]

According to this kingdom logic, if we want to be seen, we should purpose to really *see* others. If we want to be heard, we should listen, *really* listen, to those whose voices haven't been heard. If we want to be loved, we should knock ourselves out loving the unlovable. Though Jesus placed no particular value on garnering the admiring eye of others with our firm thighs or perky breasts, he really did knock himself out reminding us to turn our young and middle-aged and old faces toward those whom his Father loves, especially those on the world's so-called margins.

In the end, the reality of the aging situation effectively dissolves any illusion that this life—or the next one, for that matter—is all about us. As we die to ourselves, whether purposefully or kicking and screaming, we relinquish whatever power we might have had to attract attention with our appearances. When we do it *willingly*, we live into Jesus's good will for us. We make more room for others to be seen and heard and known and loved.

***

I believe that truth needs to be fleshed out. It's not enough to *believe* it; we need to actually put it into practice if it is to set us free. My commitment to wear bathing suits for the next four or five decades, despite the predictable opinion of more attractive others, is one way to live out reality. A strategy to put flesh—wonderful bouncy flesh—on the bones of what it is I say I believe.

My sweet Gigi, who eschewed our shared solar nemesis, never learned how to swim. For a series of summers, she'd enlist each of her four grandchildren to teach her. Gigi's sturdy green one-piece swimsuit was trimmed with the obligatory old-lady skirt. Her thick white rubber swim cap, adorned in feathery floral patterns, buckled under her sixty-seven-year-old chin. Grabbing the silver rail mounting the side of the ladder, she'd gently ease herself down to stand in the shallow end of the swimming pool. Hesitantly, at my instruction, Gigi would lean back, nervously laughing, and try to float. I'd hold her up above the water. Reminding her to fill her lungs with air. Encouraging her to relax. But she never relaxed. She never floated. She never swam.

Today when our family is together we still laugh about how hard she tried. Gigi laughs the hardest.

I can't say for sure why Gigi identified the sun as mortal enemy No. 1. I'm now making a mental note to ask her the next time I see her. Was it because she understood that melanoma, like my mom has now, can result from too much sun exposure? Or was it because she knew the sun would weather a woman's face and increase wrinkles?

Though it may be hard for some of us to tease the two apart, it matters deeply. When our behavior is determined by others' opinions of us—because, really, those wrinkles aren't *really* hindering anyone's living—we squander our energies by thinking too much (even when we have low self-esteem) of ourselves.

We experience real freedom as we think of ourselves less. For me, that will mean wearing bathing suits that expose my jiggly thighs for a very long time.

If you are young and gorgeous, and maybe have aspirations to be *America's Next Top Model*, and accidentally picked up this book at your grandma's skilled nursing facility or your mother-in-law's home, I completely understand that this whole setup seems unsavory. For those of us who want to age with grace, though, there's real promise as we choose this Jesus-way. As we begin to embrace the inevitable losses inherent in aging, we're freed up for the kind of self-giving love for which we were made.

Notes

1. C. S. Lewis, *Mere Christianity* (1952; New York: HarperCollins, 2001), 129.
2. Timothy Keller, *The Freedom of Self-Forgetfulness: The Path to True Christian Joy* (Chorley, England: 10 Publishing, 2012), 32.

Nancy Stafford

Nancy is known to millions as Andy Griffith's law partner on TV's *Matlock*. She has been a series regular on six TV series, including *St. Elsewhere*, and stars in numerous films. She is the author of two books, *The Wonder of His Love* and *Beauty by the Book: Seeing Yourself as God Sees You*. Nancy is chair of SAT-7 Women for Middle East Hope, to bring awareness to the suffering of women in the Middle East and North Africa. Of all her roles, her favorites are wife to Larry Myers, stepmom to beautiful Katie, and grandma to fourteen-year-old Blake.

Life in High Def

I've been an actress since my mid twenties, starting in soap operas shot on videotape, followed by a zillion prime time series and TV movies shot on film. Then my fifties hit—along with the savage scrutiny of high-definition television. It's just wrong! All those decades when my skin was like dew and you could pop a quarter off my cheek, *then* I could have withstood the extreme close-ups. But now? Every nook and cranny, slackness and shadow are on display. What happened to my jawline? It used to be lovely.

Talk about humbling—I think I look fine for my age until I see the final production, often projected across an enormous twenty-by-fifty-foot movie theater screen, and I'm horrified. Who is that old lady? When did my mother start acting?

I don't look like I feel. I feel as young as I did in my thirties, spontaneous, engaged, and vibrant. How I feel doesn't match how I look. That's the injustice.

A few years ago, I was the host of a series on living a natural lifestyle—health, nutrition, holistic wellness for body, soul, and spirit. I was excited. I believe in this message. I live this lifestyle. This is so *me*. Then I caught a glimpse of my mid-fifties face lit by the fluorescent light directly above. Yikes! So of course, I decided I needed Botox—immediately.

I'd sworn I'd never succumb to the knife, let alone paralyze my facial muscles or fill my crevices with plumping agents. But that crease between my eyes every time I furrowed my brow was looking deep enough to hold a three-day rain. It didn't communicate "I'm sincere when I say this," it read "I could snap you like a twig! I'm furious at everyone and everything! Back off!" I told the doctor to give me the tiniest smidge of a dose, just enough to soften things, but not so much anyone would notice.

Film is forever. When you see me on camera in this eight—*count 'em*—eight-episode series, I deliver this dialogue, "We all need to live as naturally as we can" with my eyebrows perched so high they nearly touched my hairline. You could ice-skate on my forehead; it was frozen solid. For the next several months I'd tell my husband, "Honey, I really mean it. I'm furious!" as he looked at my perfectly placid face and just shrugged. Sure, you are.

Look, we've heard from women and ad campaigns "I've earned these wrinkles" or "They're marks of a life well-lived" or "They're symbols of laughter and joy." Yeah, yeah, yeah. I just don't want to see them on *me*, on film, forever!

Which leads to the question: If I weren't on display for all to see on one hundred–inch ultra HD TVs and multiplex theater screens, would I care so much? Dunno.

There's a lot to be said for high def with its increased number of pixels, progressive scanning, and color enhancement. HDTV was astounding and revealing when it was introduced. And new systems, evolving at breakneck speed, are being unleashed on the masses in our global quest for higher resolution. Audiences want realism.

Blah, blah, blah. That raised freckle on my face, once easily covered with concealer and blurred with the welcome graininess of 35-millimeter film, is now in razor-sharp focus on exhibition for the whole world to see. With vivid clarity, we see things exactly as they are.

That's the thing about HD: everything is exposed, crystal clear, revealing every pore, flaw, nuance, shadow, and slight imperfection. It's also how God sees us, warts and all. That digital image reveals everything on the surface, just as the searing light of God reveals all that's hidden beneath it in our hearts and minds. We're laid bare, nothing to soften reality, nowhere to hide, imperfections revealed.

I want to hang on to the image I have of my face and body from my thirties, forties, even my fifties. Then the truth hits me. I also want to hang on to that image I have of who I think I am inside. Or who I believe that I have to be. Perfect. There, I said it.

We women are relentlessly bombarded by unrealistic and unattainable expectations. We have to be a super success in our careers and supermom at home. To be a spiritual giant by day and a bombshell to our husbands by night. To be thin, pretty, fashionably hip, and eternally youthful. We are expected, and we expect ourselves, to be perfect.

Women have always been busy, but we're trying to do it all, have it all, all at the same time, and do it all perfectly.

Grow your financial portfolio and organic Swiss chard.

Manage the office team of twenty and the soccer team of sixth graders.

Create gluten-free snacks for the kids' classroom and Christmas dinner (and décor) to rival Martha Stewart.

Reduce your carbon footprint and your expanding waistline.

We expect to do it all with grace and ease, our faces reflecting the placid tranquility of a Trappist monk, unfurrowed, with nary a wrinkle in sight. Which brings me back to Botox.

Like my interior life, I realize that too often I've tried to put my best (read: most perfect) foot forward, mask the real me through Botox and antiaging everything. I want to appear a certain way to the world, to look the way I think I *need* to look. It just doesn't always work. That doesn't mean I won't try again someday to freeze or fill or even surgically refurbish. Who knows?

I believe aging is a gift. I care for this one body and one face. I'm free to choose a skin-care regimen to hydrate and enhance elasticity, to use injectables, or cutting-edge medical treatments like lasers, or even surgery. Or maybe I fall somewhere in between.

We can age on our own terms, instead of stressing about what is "lost" when we look in the mirror and get an HD perspective: a clearer, sharper picture.

Celebrate *you*, and get excited about all you've experienced, accomplished, and enjoyed. Get excited about all the adventures, wisdom, and wonder yet to come. Smile and laugh! Your joy and positivity will be absolutely infectious and make you more radiant and beautiful than any laser or Botox.

Would I change things about my face? Truthfully, yes. I'd like to look the way I did in my forties or even my fifties. But I wouldn't want to be that person anymore.

I'm grateful for all I've walked through in these past two decades, even—no, especially—the high def times, the unforgiving, revealing, harsh realities of dreams dashed, pain survived, and loved ones lost. Because those glaringly stark times have grown me up, made me stronger, wiser, more humble and grateful, more empathetic, and more others-focused. I've learned that the *me* God loves is not the prettied-up, picture-perfect version, but the honest-to-goodness, real me. And those glaringly harsh times in life have grown my dependence on and faith in the One who reveals all. So finally, free of comparisons and striving for perfection, we allow him to reveal his deeper desire for us as he gracefully transforms us into the image of the truly Beautiful One.

The truth is, high def, with its unforgiving crispness and clarity, simply reveals the surface, but not the substance. The wisdom of getting older is the reality that what's on the surface is fleeting, but what God is creating is forever.

When I finally make peace with the physical imperfections HD reveals, then something remarkable happens. He lovingly fills me with himself, gently diffuses my fears, and softens my edges.

Better than Botox.

Leslie Leyland Fields

Leslie has been writing and publishing most of her life, yet like many writers, she is often visited by doubts and insecurities about the validity of her vocation. (Can story really stop bombs or feed the starving?) Sometimes the muse-attack turns personal as well. (How can you write anything about that? Who wants to hear from you anyway?) Here, Leslie confronts both of these through her turn on a stage.

I Lay Down My Doubts, I Take Up My Pen

This is my favorite scene. I crouch excitedly in the wings, settle my fur, and wait. *On!* I drop to my knuckles, bound four-legged onstage, singing "shoo be doo shoo be daa" and bobbing to the beat along with twenty-five others dressed in the same black "fur," faces painted with thick layers of makeup. On cue, my son and I begin throwing a pair of boots around, and then I leap onto a stool and pound on an antique typewriter in rhythm to the doo-wop beat. Then our shining moment of glory arrives. The spotlight turns its bright gaze on my two sons and me, and we hop onto a table for ten seconds of mayhem while the rest of our ape family tears and shreds the human campsite, all while singing our throats out.

One winter, I spent nearly every evening squatting, singing, pounding my chest, and picking nits from my gorilla children. Our community theater in Kodiak, Alaska, performed the Broadway musical *Tarzan*, complete with flying leopards and butterflies, apes hanging from vines, and Tarzan himself swinging across the jungle canopy. My part was much more lowly. I was simply one of the tribe, singing backup to the leads as we nestled in the jungle or excitedly "ee-ahah-ing" during a fight.

At fifty-seven, it was thoroughly humbling. The other cast members were, on average, thirty years younger, people with limber knees and bendy spines. I traded heels for bare feet, skirts for ragged fur, words and essays for grunts. Rehearsals were grueling. In one scene, I leapt from a five-foot platform. In another scene, my one-hundred-pound son hopped on my back while I spun and danced. My thighs ached every night. But even as I went home massaging my calloused knuckles and knees, I remembered why I loved theater and this particular story so much: theater is incarnational. Nothing human is spared, even when playing an ape. Muscle, joint, gut, knuckles, heart, tongue, breath, and mind—all are called into play to lay down oneself to embody another.

But this wasn't the real challenge. Halfway through the rehearsals, the world turned. ISIS had been rampaging across the Middle East, destroying historic villages and artifacts, visiting a kind of terror and barbarism against Christians previously unknown in our lifetimes. But then the beheadings started. I could not escape the image of the orange-suited Coptic Christian men kneeling before their black-masked executioners.

During those days I wept, prayed, felt guilty for my freedoms and my comfortable life; and at night, I was back on my hands and knees, singing "shoo-wop-de-wop." In light of such evil on the world stage, our efforts on our local stage felt frivolous and puerile. How could I justify our make-believe world when brothers and sisters in the faith were being driven from homes, tortured, killed? What good was our silly play against such hate? I despised our efforts and wanted to quit.

The question was not new to me. When my daughter, Naphtali, graduated from college, she moved to El Salvador where she lived alone in a concrete row house in a small city. She worked for an NGO committed to addressing El Salvador's endemic rates of domestic violence. Every other day, Naphtali, alone, would walk or jump on the back of a truck and grind down mud roads to three tiny villages strung along the washed-out tracks. The families were subsistence farmers who lived in dirt-floor huts dizzied with chickens and hungry dogs. Some of the women could not read; all the women bore many children, who worked in the corn and bean fields. Men wanted sons, not daughters. Her assignment was to gather women and young people into groups that would meet weekly. The women would be given microloans and taught how to manage them. In addition, Naphtali would use theater workshops to help the women and youth unravel the vicious cycle of violence. I worried about her safety, and I wondered, What could theater do against such poverty and oppression?

The question has come on the heels of every tragic headline: the Sandy Hook massacre, the Orlando nightclub bombing, the shooting of African American congregants at a prayer meeting in a Charleston church. I pick up my sorrowing hands and try to write. But in the face of such evil, what good is my own tiny art? What value is a frail craft of words sent out on such a terrible black sea?

~

I flew down to El Salvador twice in those two years, standing with my daughter on the truck as it growled its winding way to the thatched bamboo houses. One of those days we went to a party Naphtali had planned for weeks, an "intercultural fiesta" she called it. I was part of the program. We would share our lives and learn from each other.

"They'll dress up as much as they can," my daughter told me. So I dressed down: a plain cotton dress from Walmart, a plastic necklace, and old vinyl sandals.

It was nearly ninety degrees. Naphtali led the fifty who had gathered, women and children and even a few men, in a game of charades, which they had never played before. We took turns. The women acted out their lives in the villages, and I did the same for my life in Alaska. For "work," they stood in a row and swung their arms gently back and forth. I watched silently, then "Hoeing corn!" I shouted out, while my daughter translated. They grinned.

For my turn, I mimed standing in a skiff and pulling in a net heavy with fish while they watched in amused silence. Because they had heard about this already from my daughter, they guessed "Fishing!" When I pantomimed church, I bent my head to pray, I lifted my hands to worship, and I enacted Communion. They shouted "prayer!" "Praising God!" "Communion!" with the excitement of recognition.

The women had practiced songs and skits they'd written themselves.

One skit was about a girl born to a poor mother. The mother decided to pass her daughter off as a boy so she would be valued. The daughter grows up as a son. No one knows her true identity. One day she solves a crucial problem for the community and afterward reveals her true identity. She is accepted and valued by the male leaders of her village.

I stood sweating in the hot sun in a cotton dress, acting out my life, watching these women act out theirs. They were awkward. They mumbled their lines, shyly glancing and smiling at the audience. They had never acted before. No one had ever helped them tell their stories before. They didn't even know they had stories to tell. But that day, standing on a dirt stage, they saw themselves; their children saw them; we saw each other.

I didn't quit *Tarzan* that long winter. I couldn't. The play is about our response to those who are different from us. It's about a gorilla mother taking a human child into her home because the child has neither mother nor home. The gorilla father rejects the boy—until the end, when it's too late. A gun is involved. A tragic death, love is born, the guilty are caught, and at the close, two separate worlds are joined into a single family. The audience cried and cheered.

The entire town needed that musical that winter. "Beauty can save the world," Dostoevsky has famously written. I still want to protest. Can art defuse bombs, mend the blasted bodies of children, heal the blindness of misogyny? I am learning that the answer is sometimes "yes." Even simple pantomime opens our eyes to one another, revealing the stranger as our neighbor. Beauty and the truths it reveals builds bridges between faiths, cultures, genders, classes, and in our play, even between species. I suspect that terrorists and the violent must vigilantly guard their hearts against it. Music and dance could enlighten and humanize. Tender, true movies could loosen the grip on a gun. Theater could reveal that the "other" is much like you. Thoreau asks, "Could a greater miracle take place than for us to look through each other's eyes for an instant?"

Since the play, I have packed up my impotence; I will no longer host those paralyzing doubts that question the value of art and my own fumbling efforts. I will not give in to feelings of futility. The day I write this, a suicide bomber blew up twenty-two people in Manchester, England, among them mothers, fathers, teenagers, and eight-year-old Saffie, whose radiant smile pierces all who see her. In one photo she wears a school uniform, her blunt black bangs framing her enormous eyes.

I write now, here for hours and hours, until the edge of morning so you can see the women on the village stage, the orphaned boy alone in the jungle, Saffie and her bright brown eyes. I will keep on writing—for all of them.

Jennifer Grant

Jennifer is the author of six books, mother of four, and wife to one. Parts of this essay are based on a chapter in her memoir on midlife, *When Did Everybody Else Get So Old? Indignities, Compromises, and the Unexpected Grace of Midlife.* A former columnist for the *Chicago Tribune*, she has been a regular contributor to *Aleteia For Her* and Christianity Today's *Her.meneutics* as well as several other publications. She lives in the Chicago suburbs with her husband, children, and two rescue dogs. Find her online at jennifergrant.com.

Pay Attention to
What Makes You Cry

The doors of our refrigerators, once a gallery of finger-painted artwork and soccer snack schedules, are now clean and spare. Minivans have been traded in for something sleeker or have become the property of our teenagers. Hair is graying around the temples—if it's not completely silver—and the lines around our eyes point to decades of concentration, of laughter, of pain.

We have, for better and worse, figured out the shape and scope of our adult lives. We recognize the trade-offs we have made—career for family, or vice versa. We know who our friends are; our friendships are reliable, time-tested, seasoned.

But that steadiness often makes us feel stuck and we begin to feel a growing desire to bring something new into the world, and that something usually *doesn't* require a diaper bag. We get flashes of insight: "Hey, I could do that!" or "I always wanted to . . ." or "Remember how I was so good at . . ." These thoughts energize and sometimes frighten us and we aren't quite sure which path to take.

Adapted and reprinted with permission from Jennifer Grant's book, *When Did Everybody Else Get So Old?* (Herald Press, 2017). All right reserved.

A few years ago, I was weaving around the maze of cramped aisles in the shoe section at a department store when my cell phone rang. It was Mary, a friend with whom I've shared the deepest parts of my life for more than twenty-five years. Her voice shook; I knew she was in tears. I sat down, awkward and scrunched on a low stool, as other shoppers picked through the boxes of snow boots and sneakers around me. She told me she'd just finished reading Richard Stearns's *The Hole in Our Gospel* and, for the first time in her life, she felt compelled to engage with people who are affected by the AIDS pandemic in sub-Saharan Africa.

"I just never knew the scope of it," she said.

"What are you going to do?" I asked.

"I don't know," she said. "*Something.*"

Since then, she *has* done something. She's been to Ethiopia. She's brought formula and other supplies to orphanages there, educated herself about HIV/AIDS, and addressed local women's groups about extreme poverty. A few years after I got her call in the shoe section, she and her husband adopted a toddler from Ethiopia, a child who had been orphaned by AIDS. My dear friend's life changed in midlife. Her realm of influence expanded from that of a woman focused on raising her family in the pleasant Chicago suburbs to advocating for people on the margins, both here and abroad. Her family portrait reflects this change. But how did she decide?

A few years ago, I was in the Bay Area and attended a friend's church. The priest who gave the homily that day preached on the parable of the ten virgins (Matthew 25:1–13). It was one of those sermons that seemed to be precisely what, as a person edging out of my forties, I needed to hear.

In this parable, Jesus says the kingdom of heaven will be like ten bridesmaids who take lamps to await a bridegroom at night. Five are wise and bring extra oil for their lamps. Five are foolish and do not; their lamps run out while they are waiting. The foolish ones ask the others to borrow a bit of oil, but the wise ones refuse, telling them to go shopping and "buy some for yourselves" (Matthew 25:9). (This hardly seems fair. Were any shops open at that hour?)

But off they go and, unfortunately, while they are away, the bridegroom finally arrives. He welcomes the five wise bridesmaids into the wedding feast and bolts the door behind them. When the "foolish" ones return from their shopping trip, he won't let them in.

Sitting in the back of that unfamiliar church, I thought about the losses, the moments of scorching insecurity, the slammed doors, and the missed opportunities I'd had during my forties. Sometimes I'd been like the wise bridesmaids, and sometimes like the foolish ones.

There were times when I wasn't present with my whole self, but instead was blinded by self-consciousness, anxiety, or the sting of envy. Times when I didn't even know *why* I was crying. In what ways had I blinded myself to injustice and the needs of my neighbors? When had I been unprepared? What oil hadn't I shared with my children? My husband? What opportunities had I missed to serve others in my community and around the world?

The priest told us to cast aside excuses, fears, and regrets and move forward with "gumption and resolve." *Be engaged. Be prepared. Leave regrets behind.* This was an exceptionally good message for me at midlife. Now isn't the time to make excuses. It's time to move on, with hope.

But how and with what? I found myself back with the questions I asked myself about my friend's adoption decision.

In *A Crazy, Holy Grace*, Frederick Buechner writes,

> Whenever you find tears in your eyes, especially unexpected tears, it is well to pay the closest attention.
>
> They are not only telling you something about the secret of who you are, but more often than not God is speaking to you through them of the mystery of where you have come from and is summoning you to where . . . you should go to next.[1]

The hard truth is that the agitation, restlessness, and lump in your throat can be excruciatingly painful. Those tears aren't elegant or graceful—when we cry out, we do so in real confusion. We ugly cry, desperate for answers from God, and we wish these answers would come clearly, immediately . . . via email or text message, if you please. We are, hypothetically, willing to do whatever's required of us, but we can't stand waiting to know what it is. Making the transition into this new part of life takes time and more patience than we think we can summon.

Christiane Northrup ends her seminal work, *The Wisdom of Menopause*, with a similar encouragement: "We're waking up together, you and I. . . . But don't panic if you feel some pain. Whenever we give birth to anything important, like the new relationship with our souls that is possible at midlife, there are going to be labor pains."[2]

"There is enormous power here," Northrup writes. "We're at a turning point. . . . No one yet suspects how much we can accomplish when we go into our businesses, churches, clubs, and families and, quietly and peacefully, like the stealth missiles we are, set about changing everything for the better."[3]

We can begin again, in midlife, to stand with oil in our lamps, ready to change our communities and world, ready to participate more fully in what some call the "work of the kingdom."

And for you and for me, it may all begin when we notice what makes us cry.

Notes

1. Frederick Buechner, "The Gates of Pain," *A Crazy, Holy Grace: The Healing Power of Pain and Memory* (Grand Rapids: Zondervan, 2017).
2. Christiane Northrup, *The Wisdom of Menopause: Creating Physical and Emotional Health During the Change*, rev. ed. (New York: Bantam, 2012), 635.
3. Northrup, *Wisdom of Menopause*, 635.

Suanne Camfield

Suanne is the women's ministry director at Christ Church of Oak Brook and the author of *The Sound of a Million Dreams: Awakening to Who You Are Becoming*. She is a writer, speaker, and teacher who is passionate about seeing people live out the best pieces of who they are for the sake of God's kingdom. She lives in the Chicago suburbs with her husband and two children. Visit her at suannecamfield.com or follow her on Twitter @suannecamfield.

Enough of Not Enough

Sometimes good enough is good enough.

The words of my friend skate through my mind as I step onto the stage. It's Ash Wednesday, and I am preaching my first sermon.

A decade earlier, I had never even attended an Ash Wednesday service, but now the service is my favorite of the year. Something about the sacredness of the dust and ashes—the weight of our sin and morality so openly displayed—leaves me ingesting the goodness and grace of God in a palpable way.

This morning, I plead with God for my offering to be worthy of his glory. The music fades, I ascend three steps, a prayer for mercy on my lips, and begin:

> The beauty of this evening is that we gather as a community who carries and confesses a common story. We sit in a sacred space and give ourselves over to the truth of who we are and the truth of the God we worship. We muster the courage to look at our ashen frames and confess that we are but dust; we hold a mirror to our faces and stare intently at our sin. We acknowledge the truth that no matter how good we sometimes think we are, we are people who fall short of the glory of a holy God.

Perhaps even more than wanting my offering to be worthy of a holy God, I want the community to think I am worthy as well.

Partway through, I fumble over words I'd practiced a thousand times. "Carpe diem" becomes "carpe niem." I deliver my ending, twice. I descend the steps as tears sting the recesses of my eyes. I try to reassure myself: *Sometimes good enough is good enough.* Except I don't believe a word. Instead, I sit dusted in the weight of my ashes, covered in a blanket of shame.

Shame found me for the first time when I was seven years old, playing in a swimming pool wearing cut-off denim shorts and, from the waist up, naked. My brother David and I had ridden our bikes all over town, knocking on doors until we found someone to come out and play. We knew we'd hit pay dirt when the house with the swimming pool on the dead-end street was full of spirited hoots. No swimsuit in tow, I simply tore off my shirt and jumped in with the boys. It never occurred to me that there was anything amiss until the moment a girl in blond braids across the street, several years my junior, showed up in her pink ruffled one-piece. *Covered.*

Shame came crashing down, one colossal bucket at a time, and then covered me, clinging heavy as I dipped low under the water, determined forever not to resurface any higher than my chin. It was the first time it dawned on me: not that I was dressed inappropriately but that I was actually naked. Laughter must have ensued.

All these years later, I still cringe at the memory for I know the feeling too well. For what breeds shame like offering all that we have and all that we are, allowing others to see our naked selves, only to hear the echo of laughter?

I share this sentiment with my friend Amy after my sermon and her response punches me in the gut. "What if you embrace the truth that, at least sometimes, you're actually *not* good enough?"

My insides revolt. Who wants to embrace not being good enough?

The morning after my sermon, I woke up groggy and disappointed, the shame of mediocrity having kept me awake throughout the night. I dreaded the idea of greeting my colleagues, facing the world. I was about to head out the door when the Lord kindly reminded me of Peter.

Peter the fisherman, the disciple, the companion. Peter who denied, who failed. Peter whose defensiveness was unyielding. While his Beloved was overwhelmed with sorrow to the point of death, Peter slept. While his Rabbi surrendered with his arms outstretched, Peter fought. And then, as Peter warmed his hands by a fire, he denied his Messiah. The rooster crowed, and finally, Peter wept. The next time Peter met Jesus was on a beach by the Sea of Galilee, fish frying over the smoldering coals of a fire.

Jesus saw the depth of all that Peter was and all that Peter would do. Jesus saw both the resplendent light and the dim shadow, the broken, failed, and forgiven fragments. Jesus looked Peter in the eye and said four words that embodied both the truth of his failure and the depth of his worth. "Come and have breakfast" (John 21:12).

Peter accepted the invitation and stepped back toward Jesus and into the world once again. I needed to learn how to accept the same invitation.

When I got home after that Ash Wednesday service, my son was waiting in the kitchen. As a teenager, his affection is rare, but that night he greeted me with a warm, authentic hug. "You were great today, Mom. Like really, really great."

At the time, I wasn't able to fully receive his praise and acceptance. In the days that followed, in the depths of my inadequacy, the warmth of his embrace became a grace-filled invitation from Jesus. An invitation to rest in the One who accepts me exactly as I am.

Even in the smallest places, I began to embrace my *good-enoughness*: welcoming friends when the house was still dusty; showing up for coffee still sweaty from the gym; saying "I don't know" in front of colleagues without batting an eye. The choice to accept how God has gifted me to interact with the world, to accept my *good-enoughness* in him, has made the difference between pulling the covers over my head in the morning and standing confident on the stage once again.

A few weeks later, I stepped back on the same platform to teach the book of Mark, this time to a room full of women. Instead of allowing the shame of inadequacy to taunt me, I chose to set my mind on the burning embers of grace, glowing in the dusk of my *not-enoughness*, knowing my worth was far beyond anything I did or didn't do. I walked off the stage content with the outcome, fumbles and all, and basked in the beautiful flurry of conversation going on around me.

Embracing good enough has become less about changing my outward behavior and more about transforming my inner narrative. I believe that I can fail and still be worthy. I accept that I can mess it all up and still get out of bed in the morning. I can humbly, but also unapologetically, show my face to the world, lift my chin high, and hold my hands outstretched. I can receive the warm embrace of my son. I can accept, without embarrassment or shame, that I am truly both qualified and unqualified.

Madeleine L'Engle speaks well to this. If we believe we "are qualified, we tend to think that we have done the job ourselves. If we are forced to accept our evident lack of qualification, then there's no danger that we will confuse God's work with our own, or God's glory with our own."[1]

God's glory is so much better than mine.

The ending I repeated that night in my sermon, ironically, is worth repeating again. "In a world that often expects us to be perfect, embracing good enough gives us an opportunity to freely confess our imperfections. We can let down our pretenses and be truly honest with each other about who we are."

Never again will I believe that I am *not good enough* without also believing that God names me even more surely *good enough*. That is more than enough for me.

Notes

1. Madeleine L'Engle, *Walking on Water: Reflections on Faith and Art* (Colorado Springs: WaterBrook, 2001), 67.

Win Couchman

Win (1923–2017) spent over fifty years counseling, writing, and speaking domestically and around the world. After retirement, she and her husband spent four and a half years as missionaries. She was an avid writer, publishing several books and numerous articles. Win was married to her husband, Bob, for seventy-two years. She has left an incredible spiritual legacy to her four children, her grandchildren, great-grandchildren, and hundreds of people she touched through her incredible love for Christ and people.

The Grace to Be Diminished

Our friend Ken Weaver was a psychologist whose specialty was caring for older people whom he respected and admired. His description of what he considered to be their finest quality was "their grace to be diminished."

Even though my husband, Bob, and I have sat in the balcony of our church for forty years or so, sitting there has concerned me for the past several years. There are no railings up there, and the steep incline of the balcony meant that the back of the seats in front of us were too far down to lean against. But those were our seats, and around us were all our many pew friends. How could we ever move down to the floor level?

Three months ago, my beloved older sister fell; a dreadful full-length fall backwards onto asphalt. Three days later she died. Bob and I spoke to each other after it. When we get old, in many situations we must either act foolishly or look foolish. It may be wise to walk more slowly, carry a cane, whatever else is needed. Even if it looks foolish to onlookers, to be prudent, we must change our ways to match our season. We needed grace to be diminished. So a few weeks ago we gave up our balcony seats and moved to the main floor of the church.

Reprinted, with permission, from *Just Between Us* magazine (justbetweenus.org).

That was just the beginning. Following major surgery three years ago, I gave up my driver's license. I decided the world did not need any more violence, and I was fully aware that I had never been anything better than a borderline driver. At nearly eighty, it was time to quit. I signed off.

And one night I was asked to give up cooking. For years, we have been part of an every-six-weeks potluck and prayer evening for any missionaries who are home at the moment. These are among the richest ministry activities of our lives. We take two hours to visit and eat—homemade apple pies, Mexican casseroles, and big wooden bowls of salad with the season's freshest vegetables—and two hours to pray. Preparing and taking my part of the "pot" was, of course, a favorite aspect of the whole experience.

Then one of the women who coordinates the potlucks called me and said with winsome authority, "Win, enough already. You have been involved with these evenings for about twenty years now, I think. You have done your bit. We want you and Bob to be at every one, but you are not to bring any more food, you hear?" Only then did I realize how the slowness with which I function now, and the accompanying late afternoon fatigue, was beginning to color my anticipation with some dread.

Gladly I responded, "Okay."

But it's awkward to walk into someone's house on potluck Saturdays empty-handed just as another couple arrives loaded with goodies. In that moment, I silently look to God for the grace to be diminished.

Traveling gradually became a pain undertaken only because we could not bear to miss seeing our children who live on each coast. Our California son admonished us, "You guys pack too much. You can't manage all that weight anymore." For months after Don spoke his piece, in my head I kept laying out what we actually had to pack for our upcoming seventeen days in northern California. It was not going to be a lying-on-the-beach sort of time. We don't do that. The two and a half weeks would involve a wedding, attending two family reunions, and waiting for the birth of our second great-grandchild.

I plotted and planned. For one thing, I realized we must not take homemade prune bread to Don, nor could I afford the weight of extra reading material, which has always saved my life on planes and in guest bedrooms. My Bible and one other book were my limit. We shrunk our luggage to a garment bag and one suitcase. Our son applauded. I know I will now be a stingy packer for as long as we can travel.

I am not alone in my diminishments. My husband, Bob, is hard of hearing, with aids on both ears. Even then, he hears little of group conversation. Because of this, like many other people in our age group, he becomes silent and isolated at social functions. Short-term memory loss, too, is an embarrassing reality. Fortunately, this engineer man of mine is in great demand with all his children and grandchildren to utilize his computer skills to help them in various projects. Just now he is working with a sixteen-year-old grandson to design and produce business cards for the Montagnard refugees who have been rescued from persecution and are struggling to find a home in our American culture.

We are both taking advantage of every opportunity available to be enlarged to balance that which is shrinking. Bob constantly hones his computer skills, and we walk a brisk mile six days a week together, praying as we walk.

The new life in us, which we will be living forever, is looming larger every day. God's words are making more sense than ever before:

> That is why we never give up. Though our bodies are dying, our spirits are being renewed every day. For our present troubles are small and won't last very long. Yet they produce for us a glory that vastly outweighs them and will last forever! So we don't look at the troubles we can see now; rather, we fix our gaze on things that cannot be seen. For the things we see now will soon be gone, but the things we cannot see will last forever. (2 Corinthians 4:16–18 NLT)

Our early morning time of praise and prayer for each member of our family renews our spirits. We want to start by adoring God, so we always begin praying a page from a small devotional book that uses Scripture, then we turn the verses into praise or prayer.

This morning, after praising God for many blessings, we moved on to praying for each other and then our children and their children and their children. I kept my eyes open, tracking the morning star as it appeared to be moving in an arc in the predawn sky outside our bedroom window. I find incredible beauty in nature and I am in love with its Creator.

The Word he has written is becoming more personal and interesting all the time. Somehow the sense that a Person is talking with us gets more real. Bob and I are dead tired when he opens his Bible to read to us before we go to sleep at night. Yet we both love this time. He will say, "How about it, darling, are you awake enough for one more chapter?"

I am nearly always very sleepy, but I think if I really try, I can listen to one more chapter in Mark following Jesus through another one of his days on earth, before sleep overtakes me. So I answer, "Yes, one more chapter."

In our early eighties, God is giving us grace to live with those areas in which we are shrinking or becoming frail, for what lies ahead appears closer and more marvelous day by day.

Always

In the middle of winter two years ago, my husband and I traded relentless Alaskan storms for some Texan sun. While there, we visited Duncan's aunt. I could not stop staring for the two days we were with her: what a beautiful woman! She had thick red hair, a tiny cute figure. She wore colorful jewelry and classy clothes. She laughed wholeheartedly and often and asked my husband and me lots of questions, interested in our lives, though we live thousands of miles and a generation away from her. The day we left, out on her patio, we ate a salad lunch she had prepared, surrounded by the botanicals she tends so lovingly. Did I mention that she is ninety?

What is her secret? How does she stay so alive, so lovely, so caring about others when many her age have faded into weariness and apathy? I'm not entirely sure of her secret, but I do know something of others' secrets. Fourteen women open their deepest pockets to share their own. As the years have passed, we've started new adventures, we've ditched the weights that slow us down, and now, wiser, stronger, we know what matters most. No matter the changes, no matter what is lost or taken, together these fourteen women share what they cling to most joyfully, most fiercely.

Lynne Hybels starts us off with a life-changing discovery that offers wisdom to us all: the necessity of frivolity and beauty. **Kendra Smiley** and **Kay Warren** are both on board with that, urging us all to find joy and holy fun wherever we can. **Patricia Raybon** encourages us to keep answering our emails and our phones.

For the quiet times when we turn inward, **K. Martha Levitt** teaches us how to build stone walls when our dreams topple to the ground. **Ann Voskamp** struggles to make sense of a friend's diagnosis and finds a way to keep going forward. In "Make Me a Cake," **Elisabeth Elliot** learns that pain itself can be an offering to God. **Madeleine L'Engle** nudges us to value time and touch. **Vina Mogg**, caring for her mother with Alzheimer's, takes up watercolor painting, discovering the beauty of life's messy edges.

Some can't stand still and vow to keep moving, searching for God out in the wide world. **Paula Huston** wants to be outdoors every day of her life, while **Gina Ochsner** goes on a pilgrimage to a distant corner of the world. As **Joni Eareckson Tada** awakens one morning in pain, as she often does, she remembers again how to move through her day. **Jen Pollock Michel** invites us to make an awareness of our own mortality a part of both our life and worship. And finally, **Jill Kandel** offers a moving reflection on how we live in the shadow of our own coming deaths. What binds these various experiences and convictions together? The desire to be the kind of women who "flourish in the courts of our God" (Psalm 92:13).

Lynne Hybels

Lynne is an author and advocate for global engagement. In 2009, she started a fund-raising campaign for victims of war in the Democratic Republic of Congo, and is currently raising funds and awareness for Syrian and Iraqi refugees. Lynne hosts educational tours in the Holy Land focused on reconciliation efforts between Israelis and Palestinians, and wrote *Nice Girls Don't Change the World*. In 1975, Lynne and her husband, Bill, started Willow Creek Community Church. Lynne and Bill have two grown children and two grandchildren.

What Do You Love to Do?

Despite being able to count nine letters in the word frivolous, I knew that in the dictionary of God-pleasing behavior it was a four-letter word of the worst sort. The church environment I grew up in fell far to the right of center. If there was anything a good little Christian girl didn't want to be it was frivolous, and a grown woman? Shameful. Rest was frivolous. Play was frivolous. Music and art were frivolous. Nature was frivolous. Daydreaming was frivolous. Books were frivolous (except Bible studies and Christian self-help books).

Over the years, most of what I loved was shoved into the frivolous category. As a child, I gave away my ballet slippers, my fantasy books, and my art supplies. As an adult, I gave up whatever simple pleasures remained. I quit playing the flute so I could do something more pastor's wifely, like teaching a Bible study or leading a small group. I quit walking through forest preserves because that was clearly a waste of time. I was sure that giving up these activities was the right thing to do, but I was beginning to feel a bit stifled.

Okay, I was going stark raving mad; I was absolutely and utterly craving frivolity.

Fortunately, I had been seeing a counselor to help me understand the depression that had plagued me for years. He saw my strange craving for

what it was: a desperate need to balance the work, stress, and serious-
ness of life with beauty and pleasure.

"What do you love to do?" he asked. "What relaxes and refreshes you?"

Like most women juggling marriage, family, and vocation, it had been
years since I had considered those questions. I wasn't even close to having an answer. But in the midst of pondering those questions I turned
forty. Even in the best of times, forty can be traumatic. This was not the
best of times for me. Bill suggested I go bungee jumping in New Zealand
or drive a Harley Davidson through the Swiss Alps. I reminded him it
was my birthday celebration, not his, and asked if he would be responsible for Todd and Shauna (twelve and fifteen at the time) while I went
horseback riding at a friend's guest ranch in Montana. After enlisting
his mother to stay at our house, Bill gave me his blessing.

The drive from Chicago to White Sulfur Springs, Montana, was 1,387
miles—a nearly straight shot from the stable, conservative heartland
into the wildness of the West.

I packed my car with blue jeans and T-shirts, practiced changing a
flat tire in my garage, then stuffed my glove compartment with maps
and headed west. Twenty-four hours later I climbed up on a glassy pla-
teau in the Badlands of South Dakota, raised my fists to the sky and my
face to the sun, and screamed, *I'm free.* (Okay, I didn't really scream it,
but I felt it.)

After the Badlands, I stopped at a billboard-advertised Wild-West
shopping mall where I tried on fringed suede jackets and turquoise ear-
rings. Then I drove through the majestic pines of the Black Hills and
gawked appropriately at the faces of Mount Rushmore. I sped past the
undulating grasses of the golden plains, breathed the air of open spaces,
and felt giddy with a sense of independence I hadn't felt for decades.

I hadn't realized how desperately I needed to get out from under my
husband's long shadow. After nearly two decades of being "Bill Hybels's
wife," suddenly I was just me. I chatted with people in roadside diners
and small-town coffee shops who didn't care a whit who my husband
was or what hats I wore in real life. To them I was just a crazy woman
from Chicago who was heading—alone—to a horse ranch in Montana
for no other reason than she wanted to.

I wanted to. It had been so long since I had done anything just because I wanted to. So long since I had made an independent choice. Each morning I looked at my map and chose a particular route, because I wanted to. Each evening I selected a particular motel from a group of equally shabby options, because I wanted to. This sudden freedom to say "I want" and to live according to it was exhilarating.

One notion I'd carried for years was that women in ministry should never offend anybody. Consequently, for years I had done my best to walk, talk, dress, smile, serve, spend my money, choose my friends, cut my hair—you name it, it was on my list—in such a way that I would displease no one. Now suddenly none of it mattered.

Nobody at the Motel 6 cared if I wore the same dirty jeans for five days in a row. Nobody at the truck stop where I stopped for a cup of coffee cared whether or not I had a cheery smile on my face. Nobody wondered why I talked to this person but didn't talk to that person. For a brief window of time, I was free of the burden of people-pleasing.

I followed the empty expressway into Montana and bought cowboy boots in Bozeman. I headed north into White Sulfur Springs, then asked the locals for directions to the ranch. Twenty minutes later, as I twisted up the long gravel drive to my assigned cabin, I could barely believe I was really there, on my own, with a whole week stretching out before me.

Each morning I ambled along the river that cut like a diamond snake through the center of the ranch, then hiked through the pastures of high grass and over the hills golden with aspens. Each afternoon I rode horses with the rancher's wife. In the evening, I sat in front of the fireplace in my log cabin and wrote letters to Todd and Shauna on stationary covered with the haunting faces of she-wolves. I described the badger that stood on hind legs and hissed at me in the meadow, the cowboy who recited poetry by a campfire in the hills, the dinner of roasted corn and charbroiled steaks I shared with other city slicker guests like me.

One cold and sunny morning, the head wrangler invited me to help move seventy horses from the summer pasture to the winter pasture. "Go, round up those," he shouted as he nodded his head toward a group of horses gathered in a far corner of the pasture. "Round up those" sounded about as possible to me as flying to the moon, but my horse knew what to do; she galloped along the fence, then swung back toward the herd. Suddenly we were surrounded by the thunder of hoofs and the blur of flying manes. I felt like a character in a movie. The real me was up in the clouds, looking down on this other me—this me caught up in the wildness of swirling dust and muscled flanks and speeding cowboy hats.

I took long walks alone and inhaled the quietness like oxygen. During the previous twenty years, I had done what every good Christian is supposed to do: I had filled my life with people. The motto of our church is "People Matter to God" and I had chanted that mantra as enthusiastically as anyone. But often during the years I had fantasized about standing on the information booth in the main lobby of our church and shouting, "Would everybody please just leave me alone!"

I didn't know what was wrong with me.

I didn't understand the difference between introverts and extroverts. I didn't realize that some of us who truly do love people also need sizeable chunks of solitude. On my trip, I discovered that, for me, quiet moments are essential. They energize me and fill my soul with what I need in order to go back and engage with people. That simple understanding changed my life.

After my week at the ranch, I drove west to Montana's capital, Helena, for no particular reason except that it was there. After that I drove south into Wyoming and followed the twisting rivers of Yellowstone. I watched the sun set behind the jagged peaks of the Grand Tetons. I bought a leather backpack in Jackson Hole and visited a friend in Cody. In the foothills of the Bighorn Mountains, as I headed back toward Chicago, I sat in the middle of a country road for fifteen minutes while seven hundred head of black-and-white cattle meandered lazily past my little red car. A huge heifer ran her tongue in zigzags on my driver side window, while a cowboy on a tall black horse looked down at me through my open sunroof and laughed.

Hours later I sat by the bank of the Mississippi River, mesmerized by the swimming reflection of autumn leaves and grateful for the reminder of something I had forgotten—that the world is full of beauties and pleasures and thrills that are here for us to enjoy. Never again would I tell myself that it was wrong to enjoy them, because they are God's gifts of love to us.

Even after I returned home, I flung open new doors, and life came rushing in. I read great literature and wept, literally. I started playing Bach sonatas on my flute. I took an oil painting class and began loitering in art galleries. I learned to throw pots on a potter's wheel. I walked on the beach. I went fly-fishing. I kayaked along the Lake Michigan coastline. I bought Rollerblades and "danced" on country roads. I went out for cappuccino with my friends. Or without friends, if I felt like it, and quit apologizing for my love of lonely hours. The freedom to embrace the playful, the joyful, the beautiful—which my adult self tasted first on a road trip to the West—was like being creatively and emotionally reborn.

And what absolutely stunned me was that every time I enjoyed a simple pleasure, I sensed that God was enjoying my enjoyment. God wanted me to have lighthearted moments when I could be refreshed and feel fully alive.

C. S. Lewis wrote, "Joy is the serious business of Heaven."[1] Why aren't we more joyful people here on earth, right now? Embracing what we love to do is a way to start.

Notes

1. C. S. Lewis, *Letters to Malcolm: Chiefly on Prayer* (Orlando, FL: Harcourt, 1992), 93.

Patricia Raybon

Patricia is an award-winning author, journalist, and essayist who addresses topics of race, faith, church, work, family, spiritual struggle, and personal healing. Her books include *My First White Friend: Reflections on Race, Love and Forgiveness*; *I Told the Mountain to Move: Learning to Pray So Things Change*; and *Undivided: A Muslim Daughter, Her Christian Mother, Their Path to Peace*. A mother of two and grandmother of five, she lives with her husband, Dan, a retired educator, near Denver, Colorado.

Answer the Phone

I'm not twenty-five anymore. Or forty-five. Or even still sixty-five. But God doesn't care. It's Monday and my phone is ringing. My email box is full. My workload is steady. The harvest is ripe, as the Good Book says, and God has work for me to do. For you, too.

And that's the biggest surprise to me about getting older. *God doesn't care about age.* He needs willing workers. Thus, my biggest life questions aren't about whether I will dye my hair, buff my thighs, or get a Botox shot. It's these: Am I still willing to work? Work for God? And not stop?

I know my answers. But to be honest, before sitting down to scribble these few humble words, I never wrestled much over stages and ages of life. That's because I've always worked. And work is curious and holy, no matter our age or season, our calling or color. I used to think our best years were based on timing and talents. Both are important, to be sure. But our best years, it turns out, are based on our godly purpose—and our willingness to labor for the cause of it. As a *New York Times* article recently declared about an eighty-nine-year-old Brooklyn artist: "Her Secret to a Long Life? 'It's Good to Work a Lot.'"

I agree, but my daddy already taught me this principle early on. He didn't have sons. Instead he had "the girls"—my sister and me, born to him and my mother in the Jim Crow fifties. Growing up black in his proud household—daughters of this military veteran and his "wing-man," our mom—we were up at dawn every day, making our beds, clearing the dishes, sweeping the carpet, cleaning the bathroom, moving rocks. Literally.

This was in the sixties after fair-housing laws passed, so my hard-working parents moved our "colored" family from our beloved but cramped inner-city bungalow to a squeaky new tract house out in the sticks. It was our new beginning, surrounded by suburban sameness and rocky bare front yards. Nobody dared say we didn't belong. So Daddy roused my sister and me early one Saturday morning and asked us to collect all the rocks. He was eager to sod the yard, determined to build a suburban-worthy lawn and calm the neighbors.

Thus, I moved rocks. All day. I was fourteen and skinny and the rocks were heavy. But the sky was blue, the sun was shining, the birds were cheeping, and the work, as work tends to be, was doggone good. Working alongside, Daddy led the way, making us feel capable, if not strong. Standing in our long shadows at the end of the day, we looked across a sod-ready yard, not bitter but grinning.

"You did good," Daddy said.

"Thanks, Daddy," I said to him. "You did good, too."

This was our contract. He would teach us to survive a bad world. We would obey what he asked.

I know many will say that was wrong—that Daddy's authoritarian-ism was stifling, or maybe even abusive. But of all the things my daddy taught me, starting with the sufficiency of Christ and his cross, the sec-ond best was that work *is* a wonder. And age? It doesn't matter.

In our youth-seduced culture, aging is bemoaned and belittled. Wrinkles are reviled. Gray hairs are camouflaged. Culture clearly hasn't read the book of Exodus. Right there in the third chapter, there's Moses climbing around a mount called Sinai, tending his father-in-law Jethro's sheep. He is eighty years old. *But God doesn't care about age.*

Instead, God looks at Moses and says the kindest words this sojourner has probably ever heard. *Take off your sandals.* Meaning what? Stop wasting time on Jethro's sheep. Stop dragging your dusty flip-flops on *unholy* ground. Instead, take off your sandals before me. And then?

Get to *real* work. That's when you can change everything, Moses is told, even if he can't quite believe it.

Moses pushes back, of course. He says he's not qualified: "What if they won't believe me or listen to me? . . . I get tongue-tied, and my words get tangled" (Exodus 4:1, 10 NLT). We hear Moses today, understanding his worry, because he sounds like most of us: self-doubting, dismayed, and lacking courage.

But do you hear what Moses *doesn't* ask? Even at eighty, Moses never asks, "What if I'm too old?" He's worried about other things instead. His speech. His ability to lead those unruly people. He even begs to bring along his brother Aaron—who, at eighty-three, is no spring chicken.

Our wonder years? Moses never even frets about age. God doesn't either. So why do we?

Somehow we draw a line in some chronologic sand, arguing unwisely that, after a certain year, we'll finally become this person or achieve that goal. We dream of "retirement," a concept barely mentioned in the Bible (excepting for those Levite priests in Numbers 8:24–25). Many of us, however, still dream of the golf course or the front porch—stepping off life's stage, arguing we're too old to give more. Regarding age, however, God truly doesn't care. As the Creator of years *and* time, he advises us to "number our days," not to count down to retirement, but to "gain a heart of wisdom" (Psalm 90:12).

Thus, as the psalmist David wrote, the godly in old age will "still bear fruit," remaining "fresh and green"—flourishing "like a palm tree" (Psalm 92:12–14).

Indeed, God uses willing people at every age. The Scriptures are full of such heroes, including Deborah the warrior, Esther the queen, Ruth the gleaner, and Abigail the gorgeously intelligent discerner. But there's also the young shepherd boy David, the little servant girl of Naaman's wife (see 2 Kings 5:1–19), and the generous young lad who shared his meager lunch with Jesus, allowing the Lord to transform five barley loaves and two fish into a feast for five thousand.

All were people of purpose, and many were far older. Abraham and Sarah, at one hundred and at ninety, were charged with bearing a covenant son and parenting a nation. Noah at six hundred built the ark.

Then we see Zechariah and Elizabeth who were "both very old" (Luke 1:7) when they became the parents of John the Baptist. Anna the prophetess served in the temple until her "very old" age, watching and waiting for the Messiah. Yet when she finally saw him, she didn't kick off her shoes, sit herself down, and retire—she worked even harder, speaking about the child "to all who were looking forward to the redemption of Jerusalem" (Luke 2:36–38).

Now what about us? If we're waiting for some special decade to experience wonder, we're reading the wrong book. God doesn't care about our age.

My daddy must've known this. So on Sundays, he took us to church. He wanted us to know the God of the ages, the one who would make every moment a wonder if we would surrender all our days to him.

Which brings me finally, and gratefully, to Jesus. Yes, our Carpenter. He spent his adult life building. Then at thirty, he turned toward Galilee and changed the world. He was *the* worker of all time. Then he made us a stunning promise, that whoever believes in him would do "even "greater works" (John 14:12 NLT). And our works would be miracles. Not just moving rocks—we could move mountains (Matthew 17:20).

Jesus explains how: "because I am going to be with the Father" (John 14:12 NLT). This good news means the Holy Spirit, sent to us from Christ, will empower us, unleashing our potential to keep working for the kingdom. And not stop. That can sound hard, if we work in our own strength. The oldest woman I know, now 104 and still kicking, confirms that with this piece of advice (the best she ever gave me): "To live a good long life? Pace yourself." As she put it, "Stay busy. But let the Holy Spirit do the work." And he will.

For my part, my phone keeps ringing and, with gratitude, I keep answering. I keep joyfully answering.

I hope you will, too. Answer the phone. Then say yes. To leaning. To learning. To loving. And then every year the harvest will be sweeter. Why? God's good fruit in us.

Joni Eareckson Tada

Joni, the founder and CEO of Joni and Friends International Disability Center, is a writer and an international advocate for people with disabilities. A diving accident in 1967 left Joni, then seventeen, a quadriplegic in a wheelchair. She has written over fifty books, including *Joni & Ken: An Untold Love Story*. She has received numerous awards, including the Gold Medallion Lifetime Achievement Award from the Evangelical Christian Publishers Association. Joni and her husband, Ken Tada, have been married since 1982.

Three Turns of the Ramp

Five different friends, on five different mornings, drive me from home to work. It means four stoplights, a sharp turn onto the 101, exit, then another three lights, and a right-hand turn onto Agoura Road. There's one more light before you turn onto Ladyface Court, which winds up the hill to the International Disability Center—but I don't count that one, because there's enough room to brake long and slow up to the light.

I know every bend, every intersection of the route. I know it because each stop and turn causes a sharp jag in my back. It's why on the freeway I always ask the girls, "Could we please get out of the slow lane? The trucks have sure made it bumpy."

I may not love the drive to work, but I do love arriving.

Our receptionist recently called it "a little bit of heaven." And so it is. The center stands tall and large, reminding me of the vision that brings me here every day: *to communicate the gospel and to equip Christ-honoring churches worldwide to evangelize and disciple people affected by disability.*

Just this morning as Sandy was driving me up Ladyface, I said with a sigh and a smile, "How many people get to do something each day that literally changes lives for eternity?!"

"We do," she said with a smile into the rearview mirror.

I hit the handicap access plate by the center's front doors, which slowly swing open, and in I wheel—heading not for the elevator, but the ramp.

I always take the ramp.

Centered in the middle of the lobby, it's a slow, winding climb around the chapel to my second-floor office. And the chapel is, of course, the first place I want to visit. Yes, my secretary's waiting. Yes, there are piles on my desk demanding attention. Yes, I have an interview at 10:30 a.m. But I can't clear my head of those jags in my back until I spend a moment with God. It's a moment that always includes a word of thanks that I'm here . . . and a prayer for healing from the pain.

I proceed to the second floor, where on each of the three landings, a Bible verse has been inscribed in large flowing script on walls of soft lavender.

Three turns in the ramp. Three landings. Three verses.

The first one reminds me of my purpose—why I get out of bed, go through an elaborate morning routine to get ready for the day, and endure fresh visitations of pain on my commute to the center. It's why we're all here at Joni and Friends—to go out, find the disabled, and bring them in.

> But when you give a banquet, invite the poor, the crippled, the lame, the blind, and you will be blessed. (Luke 14:13–14)

Around the next turn in the ramp, at the second landing, the second wall speaks to me of God's provision for the task He has placed before me—and reminds me that His special favor rests on those who are weak.

> "My gracious favor is all you need. My power works best in your weakness!" So now I am glad to boast about my weaknesses, so

that the power of Christ may work through me. (2 Corinthians 12:9 NLT 1996)

And the last verse at the last turn assures me that my Lord will soon come again, gathering His scattered family and mending what has been long broken.

And when he comes, he will open the eyes of the blind and unstop the ears of the deaf. The lame will leap like a deer, and those who cannot speak will shout and sing! (Isaiah 35:5–6 NLT 1996)

That's the verse, right there on the third landing, that always brings tears. Because my time in the chapel didn't dissipate the spear thrusts in my hip and lower back. It's still there as I write these words—and yes, it's getting worse. Today may be yet another day when I work from the little bed in my office rather than from my wheelchair.

Did God hear my cry for help and healing in the chapel today? I'm sure He did. But for reasons He knows best, the throbbing persists.

How long will this pattern continue? How many more days of pain piercing me at every stoplight on my commute, following me around three slow turns of the ramp to my office? Of course I can't know that. But those verses on three successive walls, at three successive landings, painted there long before this current season of elevated physical stress, continue to speak to me, continue to illuminate the path ahead, and continue to help me keep on keeping on, for yet one more day.

First landing: "Give a banquet . . . invite the poor . . . you will be blessed."

In other words, *My daughter, keep on going in My name to the broken, discouraged, and despairing. Keep on being My hands and feet and eyes and ears for those who are without. Do this as long as you are able.*

Second turn: "My gracious favor is all you need. My power works best in your weakness!"

My daughter, I have not forgotten your need. I have not overlooked your hurt, disregarded your pain, closed My ears to your cry for help, or in any way withheld My favor from you. I will provide for you, and I will continue to show My might through your weakest moments, honoring your faintest attempts to honor and serve Me.

And the final turn: "And when He comes . . . the lame will leap like a deer!"

I come. Watch for Me! The help for which you pray—more help than you can conceive—is just around the corner. Just over the horizon. Can you see? The clouds are already beginning to part. I am coming with gifts of health and strength and joy and life like an artesian fountain. I am making all things new.

Three turns in the ramp, three landings, three reminders from the Word that is forever fresh and new. What's life all about for me in these days of sometimes blinding pain?

Mission, provision, and hope. A task that still needs doing, a promise that still holds true, and a hope that keeps me glancing toward the horizon.

For now, for today, it is enough.

Ann Voskamp

Ann is a home-educating mama to seven exuberant kids, and author of four *New York Times* best sellers: *The Broken Way, The Greatest Gift, Unwrapping the Greatest Gift,* and *One Thousand Gifts: A Dare to Live Fully Right Where You Are,* which has sold more than one million copies. She was named by *Christianity Today* as one of fifty women most shaping culture and the church today. Ann partners with Compassion International as a global advocate for needy children. She blogs at annvoskamp.com.

How Can I Not Keep Reaching Out?

When I wake up the morning of my fortieth birthday, I couldn't care a rat's bony hind leg if the sun ever shows its face again, or if there's a half-price sale on boots down at The Bay or if I ever get to trek through Iceland or if the kids pick up whatever's exploded like volcanic debris all over the house. You can forget there's any light in living, in your soul. You can find it hard to remember. Your pen can run out of blue ink and you can lose that gratitude journal and ask me how I know. I can get God-Alzheimer's.

I roll over, bury my head under the pillow. Anxiety can come out of nowhere. Get busy, get distracted, and you can forget God. Forget God, and you lose your mind and your peace. Forget God, and all you remember is anxiety. Anxiety can give you God-Alzheimer's. Forget the face of God, and you forget your own name is Beloved. *Beloved, you are the re-membering people. Find your feet. Find His face—His broken-wide-open heart of communion.*

I lie there for what feels long, and not nearly long enough. The hands of the clock on the wall, they keep following the invisible, trying to track it.

I can hear the dog slurping from that one-handled pot we demoted to a water dish.

A cousin, she'd called at midnight. We've got whole yellowing photo albums of us with big bangs and pop-bottle glasses. Her third-year university son who'd been baptized and shared his testimony before the whole congregation, he'd just decided he's actually an atheist. He's done with the supposed flimsy fairy tales. You can howl with a mother at midnight and feel the weight of darkness filling your moans.

My ninth-grade science teacher, Mr. Biesel, said you can't see time. Time can only be represented by change, by the way things move and change. I lie there on a birthday morning, not wanting to get out of bed, as if I can change, and still stop time. Middle-age birthday and—oh, how did it all become so late so soon? *Is anything you're doing here adding up to anything that matters? And in the end, is what you've chosen ultimately about Christ and His kingdom?* If not, then no matter what you've chosen, it won't matter at all.

That cross I'd penned onto my wrist the day before, it's about rubbed off. I've got no bloody idea at all how you take this dare. How can all the bad brokenness be broken with good brokenness? How do you live cruciform—and be broken and given into a kind of communion?

There's a mama round the corner from the farm, they say she's been up for days rocking that brand-new daughter of hers who the doctors conceded last week has a fatal disease. What in God's good name was the clock on her wall saying?

I'd sat up late the night before to write back to my friend Elizabeth. We had met nearly six years ago—two mothers with nearly a dozen kids between the two of us—commiserating over houses that seemed to manufacture chaos like it was our actual business plan. I told her I was trying to remember to put my priorities on all things unseen. Told her I was trying to slay the idol of the seen, break the idols of performance, and believe the state of my house doesn't reflect the state of my soul. And she'd confirmed it's the priorities unseen—the prayers, the relationships, the love while doing the work—that hold the meaning, the merit. And she'd leaned in and asked if we could be friends for life, and I had said, "Deal," and laughed way too loud.

I couldn't have known then that Elizabeth would turn out to be unlike any other friend I'd ever had. Who else sends courage in a box and pounds of milk chocolate that would show up at the door? Who else would reach out late at night and say, "I see you, the you behind everything you're doing, and I like you—the you that just is"? Who else lived out priorities unseen—priorities that let the people around her, me, be known? I couldn't have known then that Elizabeth would be the friend for life that my life needed in ways I hadn't expected.

Then last night, Elizabeth said hospice had just started coming to the house.

How do you end up being forty-something with hospice knocking on your front door? How can God let the world break a bit like this? How is *this* all grace? How is *this* love?

I bury my head deeper into the pillow. Rub a bit at that smudged cross on my wrist . . . and yet *it is love. Who knows why God allows heartbreak, but the answer must be important enough because God allows His heart to break too.*

I reach for the pen on my nightstand, the way I've reached for ink to count a thousand ways He loves me, the way ink's been the cheapest of medicines. But now—can the ink be lived, branded onto the skin, how could it leave the page and lead a way through pain?

The ink would start right there on my scarred wrist, right where part of me wanted to kind of die, and not in the saving way, and somehow there is good brokenness that grows out of every scar and wound we will ever suffer. *Draw one line vertically down my wrist, right over scars.* The question of evil and suffering is answered in the breaking of God's own heart too. *Draw another line horizontally across my wrist, breaking scar lines with cross lines.* Our broken hearts always break His. It's the quantum physics of God: Your one broken heart always splits God's heart in two. You never cry alone.

And still—your brokenness can feel like a tomb you can't quite claw yourself out of. Is the most painful kind of tears the kind no one can see, the kind where your soul weeps alone? You can feel the corners and edges of you withering with the weight of scar tissue on your own soul.

The flannel sheets feel like grave clothes. *How long can I refuse to move?* Exhale.

Maybe air isn't all that keeps you alive. There's a cross that's helping me breathe. It's reminding me, re-forming me, and I'm so insufferably forgetful. I try to remember that grace swallowed with courage is elemental to living.

Inked cross bleeding into my arms. Swallow down His grace. What He gives is enough—enough courage to move up out of bed. *One small step for a woman, one giant leap for her sanity.* The woman with broken kids, the friend with dying friends, the ache of a broken heart. Just take the first step. And then the next step. Courage is reaching out and taking just a bit of that iron-nail grace.

I make my hand reach out, the one with that penned cross, make that hand reach out and turn on the light. The way you always find the light in the dark is to make your hand reach out.

Find an old flannel shirt in the bottom dresser drawer, pull on the worn threads over outstretched arms. So if we're all born with our hands clenched into these tight fists—what does it mean to live with hands wide open, hands reached out?

How in the world will you live with your one broken heart?

A book sits in a pond of light on the edge of the dresser. In the kitchen, a crumbling handful of yesterday's cookies sits on a plate. When I wander out to the red mailbox at the end of our lane, I leave a book and brown paper bag of cookies for the mail carrier.

On the way in, I will myself to pick a bunch of zinnias and glads from the weedy, tangled patch masquerading as a garden. I say their name out loud as I pick—"glads, glads, glads." *Remind me. Rewire me.* That cross on my wrist begs like a prayer:

Become cruciform. Like a cross. Transform.

If it is true that to become cruciform, to let your life become shaped like a cross, is to become more fully human—and most fully like Christ—then this is the work most urgent, most needed.

The dirt in the garden feels like gritty grace there underneath fingernails. I've got no idea what made me think of taking these flowers to the nursing home in town right then, and there isn't a bone in my weary body that wants to do it. There are days you don't want to keep breathing—but your body doesn't forget how and it does it anyway.

Your body breathes for you anyway. And you are part of a body always. There's a cross that is your backbone, and all you have to do is reach out your arms.

Find water for the zinnias. Reach for the Mason jars for vases.

The way to find the light in the dark is to make your hand reach out—reach out in thanks, reach out in giving. And maybe your hand has to reach out so your heart keeps beating—so someone else keeps breathing. Maybe this can be a way to keep breaking the bread and reaching out to pass it down, right through brokenness.

How can I not keep reaching out while I'm still alive?

Elisabeth Elliot

Elisabeth (1926–2015) was a Christian author and speaker. Her first husband, Jim Elliot, was killed in 1956 while attempting to make missionary contact with the Huaorani of eastern Ecuador. She later spent two years as a missionary to the tribe members who killed her husband. Returning to the United States after many years in South America, she became widely known as the author of over twenty books and as a speaker. Elliot toured the country, sharing her knowledge and experience, well into her seventies.

Make Me a Cake

During the months of my second husband's terminal illness, I sometimes felt I could not bear one more day of seeing him suffer, or one more visit to the doctor who would tell us terrible things that must be done next—things like removing the lower jaw because of the lip cancer, or castration because of the prostate cancer. Everything in me said NO NO NO NO. Add's suffering became mine. The wee hours were filled with nightmarish images of things far worse than death, and I was afraid. What to do?

The answer came to me.

"Offer it up."

My eyes had been opened to this possibility through the reading of Evelyn Underhill's classic, *The Mystery of Sacrifice*. I had never before been taught the deep truth of making all of life an oblation, but this little book had come into my hands just three months before we discovered my husband's illness. I do not know what I would have done without it.

Offer up *what*? I felt like the destitute widow of Zarephath, about to use the last of the flour and oil which stood between her son's and her own starvation, when along came Elijah and told her to bake him a cake first. Because it was the word of the Lord, she obeyed. The effects of that obedience went far beyond her imagination. "There was food for him and for her and her family for a long time. The jar of flour did not give out nor did the flask of oil fail, as the word of the LORD foretold through Elijah" (1 Kings 17:15–16 NEB).

It was only a vaguely remembered fragment of a poem by Amy Carmichael that brought to mind the analogy between suffering and the poverty of the widow of Zarephath. I give it here in full:

Nothing in the House

Thy servant, Lord, hath nothing in the house,
Not even one small pot of common oil;
For he who never cometh but to spoil
Hath raided my poor house again, again,
That ruthless strong man armed, whom men call Pain.

I thought that I had courage in the house,
And patience to be quiet and endure,
And sometimes happy songs; now I am sure
Thy servant truly hath not anything,
And see, my song-bird hath a broken wing.

* * *

My servant, I have come into the house—
I who know Pain's extremity so well
That there can never be the need to tell
His power to make the flesh and spirit quail:
Have I not felt the scourge, the thorn, the nail?

And I, his Conqueror, am in the house,
Let not your heart be troubled: do not fear:
Why shouldst thou, child of Mine, if I am here?
My touch will heal thy song-bird's broken wing,
And he shall have a braver song to sing.[1]

I had nothing in the house. Nothing except this pain. Pain—an offering? What could the Lord possibly make of that?

"Make me a cake." In other words, Elijah said: There *is* one thing you can do. Even from your poverty, you can give me something. It may not seem like much, but it is the very thing I need. If you will give it to me I can do something I could not do without it.

"The sacrifices of God are a broken spirit: a broken and a contrite heart, O God, thou wilt not despise" (Psalm 51:17 KJV).

So, as best I could, I offered it up.

That was fifteen years ago. It has taken me a long time to assimilate this great lesson. I have not yet mastered it. But my understanding of sacrifice has been transformed. It has also transformed my life. The emphasis now is not on loss, privation, or a price to be paid. I see it as an act of intelligent worship, and as a gift God has given me to give back to Him *in order that He may make something of it.*

When Add died in September of 1973, the Lord in His mercy helped me to see a little more clearly in my second widowhood what I had only dimly descried in the first: a gift, a call, and a vocation, not merely a condition to be endured. Paul's words came alive: "Each one must order his life according to the gift the Lord has granted him" (1 Corinthians 7:17 NEB).

So it was the Lord who had put into my hands this gift of widowhood. Is this the little "cake" You need from me, Lord? Then I'll bake it for You, Lord. Please have it.

And what next? "I will offer . . . the sacrifice of thanksgiving" (Psalm 116:17 KJV). It is wonderfully comforting to be absolutely sure that we do the will of God. Here is one matter about which there can be no doubt: "Be thankful, whatever the circumstances may be. For this is the will of God for you in Christ Jesus" (1 Thessalonians 5:18 PHILLIPS).

Notes

1. Amy Carmichael, "Nothing in the House," in *Toward Jerusalem* (Copyright 1936, Dohnavur Fellowship). Published by Christian Literature Crusade, Inc., Ft. Washington, Pennsylvania, 44.

Vina Mogg

Vina is a recent empty nester learning to fly on her own after raising four children. She is launching into various workshops across the continent and beyond (including Harvester Island, Alaska, and Puy l'Eveque, France) in writing and painting to find her wings. She is an advocate for caregivers after caring for her mother with Alzheimer's for the past ten years and is working on a memoir, *A Light in the Fog*, about her caregiving journey. Various stories about Alzheimer's and caregiving can be found on her blog, seaglasslife.com, and have been published in *HuffPost, Grand* magazine, and grandparentslink.com.

Messy Edges

I remember the first time I held a watercolor brush in my hand. There was something therapeutic about the weight of it between my fingers, the shape of the brush tapering at the end just so. A brush could carry the load of pigment and water mixed together so its touch released a blush of color onto the paper. I started with one color, a permanent rose, but when it came time to work in the second, Aurelian yellow, my image blotted on the page. I was frustrated. How could I control the spread of color?

My instructor glanced over my shoulder. She was a local artist whose work—loose, free, and transparent—I had admired for years.

"You're trying to control it too much," she offered. "It's okay to let the colors run together. Let the edges get messy. That's the beauty of it."

I laid my brush down and looked up at her in tears. "You don't understand," I said. "Messy describes my life right now exactly."

At that time, Alzheimer's was clouding my mother's brain, slowly arresting her ability to think, to communicate, to remember. Mom, previously an outgoing, animated schoolteacher, now had trouble recalling a conversation, or remembering if she had eaten, or that she had been hospitalized for a week with the flu.

"I want to go home," she would say, after nearly every conversation.

"Mom, you live with us now. We sold your house years ago."

"Home," she would repeat. "Home, to the Philippines. I have to take care of my mother."

As my mother's Alzheimer's gradually advanced, simple things like getting her into the car, shuttling her between doctor appointments, and taking her to adult day care took so much time and patience. I was losing both. I was trying desperately to control things that were out of my control. I was not only caring for my mother, but my four children as well. My heart was guilt-ridden and burdened, caught between allegiance to my teenage children (knowing they would soon be out of the home and gone), and resentment at the consuming needs of my mother.

After a while, with much reluctance, we brought caregivers into our home, first during the day, then full-time as my mother could not be left alone. It was an extraordinarily messy time, when schedules, demands, and relationships all ran together in a blurry mess. My great escape became the Art Room, the local studio where I took weekly lessons. For those hours every week, the clock stopped. Painting eased the burden of medication schedules, physical therapy routines, and neurology appointments. They all evaporated in the joy of mixing color and creating shapes from pigment and light.

I learned to trust my heart and instincts as I let go. I let the colors on my palette push and shape themselves. I watched as the dark colors illuminated the lighter hues. Painting kept me sane in the midst of my grief, my broken heart, and my weariness.

At home, I suffered through sleepless nights, getting up every two hours to check that my mother hadn't wandered or fallen. But it wasn't all difficult. On bright days, we took sidewalk strolls, our arms interlocking. Gradually, though, as the disease progressed, the arm-in-arm walks became wheelchair rides, often beneath a canopy of oak trees.

My mother is still with me as I write this. Today, I stop when she notices a red geranium, just like the ones she used to have outside her home.

"What flower is that, Mom?" I ask her.

She looks at it and smiles. "Geranium," she whispers.

A stroke has weakened her voice and her left side and keeps her mostly bedridden, but on these walks these images bring her joy. She notices the way the shadows drift between the tree branches when the sun is overhead. She notices the flock of crows that call in the bright blue sky. These small things bring a smile to her face, a smile I wish I could capture and tuck into my memory forever.

We stop now to study an old oak tree, the tip of its gnarled branches releasing the first buds of spring. "How does it look?" I ask her.

She peers up at the sky, her small bony fingers grasping the edges of the blanket covering her lap.

"Fresh," she answers.

She smiles and time stands still. She pushes me to see beauty and wonder in every small thing, as if for the first time. My mother, even in her illness, gives me this gift, this gift of seeing. When I paint, these are the moments I try to capture. A field of sunflowers, a field of lavender. A single bloom, an iris, her favorite. I try to keep the colors pure and vibrant. I try to use brushstrokes that remain fresh and lively, not overworked. For I was holding on, too tightly, to the brush, to mom's health, to life, afraid to loosen the grip, to lose control of the things I could not control. Now I understand that beauty unfolds in the letting go, in allowing the messy edges to bleed.

Ten years have passed since that first art lesson. Ten years have passed since my mother first came to live with us. Mom barely remembers the names of my children anymore. One of my greatest fears is the day she does not remember mine. Sometimes, she plays a game with me. Feigns that she does not remember my name, pauses, then smiles, and spells it out: V-I-N-A.

This week I am working on painting an iris. A single bloom. I am pleased with the shape and the colors. The last stage of a painting is to step back, to create distance, to see it complete. I do not always recall how or why these darks were laid down or why those lights were placed just so. But I have come to trust, finally, that every blot and stroke of color is needed for the whole.

But one thing remains. I put down my brush and choose a pencil. I step near again.

In the corner, I sign my name: *V-i-n-a.*

Kay Warren

Kay, cofounder of Saddleback Church with her husband, Rick, is an international speaker, best-selling author, and Bible teacher. She is best known as a tireless advocate for those living with mental illness and HIV/AIDS, and the orphaned and vulnerable children left behind. Kay is the author of several books including *Choose Joy: Because Happiness Isn't Enough* and *Say Yes to God*, and coauthor of *Foundations: 11 Core Truths to Build Your Life On* with Pastor Tom Holladay.

Joy Is a Choice

Some people have decided that because life is absurd and there is pain in life, God must not exist. I say that *because* life is absurd and there is pain in life, I need God more than ever. If I didn't have God in my life, I couldn't survive. Yes, life is absurd. Yes, there is pain. But we run *to* God in our pain, not *away* from him.

I heard this the other day: "If something is going to be funny later, it's funny now, so go ahead and laugh about it." What a great perspective! Proverbs 15:15 says, "Every day is a terrible day for a miserable person, but a cheerful heart has a continual feast" (GW). Begin to look for the humor in your life—even if it is absurd.

A friend of mine loves to tell her most embarrassing dating moment. She met a great guy, and after they'd had a few dates, he invited her to go waterskiing with him and his brothers, whom she had never met.

After her ski run, she was trying to climb gracefully back into the boat in her cute little bikini. But as she climbed up, the bottom of her bikini got caught on a hook. As she slid into the boat, she and her bikini bottom became separated from each other. Her bikini bottom floated in the lake, while she was exposed in all her glory in front of her new boyfriend and his brothers.

If this had happened to me, I would have jumped back into the water and drowned myself! My friend? She married the guy! She says, "I figured he'd seen it all, so I might as well marry him."

When my grandmother got old, she lost muscle tone in a certain part of her anatomy, and she had a little trouble with passing gas. As she walked, she made this little toot-toot-toot sound. I would have been totally humiliated if that had happened to me, but she chose to see the humor in the situation. I remember her saying, "I am eighty years old, and if I want to toot when I walk, I will! Here I come: Toot-toot-toot!"

Going through breast cancer was not funny. The chemo I was taking guaranteed that I was going to lose all my hair. When it started to thin, I didn't want the trauma of watching it fall out in clumps, so I decided to make a preemptive strike and shave my head and start wearing a wig.

Even though I had done a lot of reading and talked to my doctor, I was just not prepared for how painful that experience would be. I can still get emotional when I'm talking about it because I have never felt more vulnerable or naked in my entire life. I did a lot of crying at first about it. But after I had worn that wig for about a year, it became less traumatic. I learned how to laugh about it.

I remember clearly one incident soon after I had finished my chemo but was still wearing my wig. I had come back to church, and I was teaching one of our women's Bible studies. It was my birthday, so all the women had loaded me down with cards and gifts. I also was holding my books and Bible, so my arms were full.

My friend Elizabeth and I were walking out to my car, and the wind was blowing pretty hard. (Can you see where this is going?) As we were walking with our arms loaded, I felt the wind catch the back of my wig. Before I knew it, my wig flew off my head and rolled end over end through the parking lot like a squirrel on the run for the border.

Elizabeth and I began to scream with laughter. Both of us ran after it but since our arms were full, the only way I could stop this tumbling wig was to jump on it. As I picked it up, we doubled over with laughter. Where is *America's Funniest Home Videos* when you need them?

About that time I saw a big SUV come very slowly toward us. A friend of mine was driving, and her eyes were huge!

"Did you see what happened?" I asked, still laughing.

"Yes! But I didn't know whether to help you or just drive on and pretend I hadn't seen a thing."

"Well, you should have helped me chase my wig!" I told her.

A few months later, I was still wearing a wig when I was asked to speak at the beginning of a women's weekend event at church. I was trying to explain to the women listening that they needed to be vulnerable. God was going to be talking to them in the upcoming days, and in order to receive what he was saying to them, they needed to let their guards down and be vulnerable before him. I told them about the time I'd lost my wig in the church parking lot and how vulnerable I had felt.

I did not plan to do this, but as I got to the place in the story when the wind took my wig off, I impulsively reached up and flipped my wig out into the audience. They shrieked. *Eeeeek!* As if I'd thrown a snake at them or something. Finally, a lady in the front row bravely picked it up and dropped it like a hot potato on the edge of the stage.

I'd already done my crying. It was time to laugh.

Laughter and tears come from the same deep well in the soul. That's why sometimes we laugh until we cry and sometimes we cry until we laugh. If you can laugh but you can't cry, you need to get some help. If you can cry but you can't laugh, you need to get some help. And if you can do neither, you definitely need to talk to a good friend or a counselor.

God intends for you to be able to weep freely and laugh uproariously, just as Jesus did. When you can recognize both the pain and the humor around you, you take another step toward knowing true joy.

Kendra Smiley

Kendra is a popular speaker who has addressed thousands of women nationally and internationally. She is a regular guest on Chicago's WMBI, Moody Radio, and hosts a daily radio show, *Live Life Intentionally,* heard on over 350 stations. She is also the author of nine books including *Live Free* and *Journey of a Strong-Willed Child.* Kendra and her husband, John, a retired military pilot, live on a farm in central Illinois. They are the parents of three grown sons, and are grandparents to ten, ages seven and under.

The Freedom of Fun

"Come on, fun seekers! It's time to go!"

I had no idea how often I spoke those words until my youngest son, then in college, pointed it out to me. "Mom, you may not realize it, but it didn't matter where we were going—to the library, to Grandma and Grandpa's house, or to the grocery store—that's what you always said to get us out of the house and into the car."

Yes, I guess I did. Why? Because I was unconsciously determined to make each and every outing an adventure. The grocery store, really? Absolutely! As we zipped through the aisles we'd think of words that rhymed with the items on our list. And the rhyming words didn't necessarily have to be legitimate. After all, Dr. Seuss made a career out of rhyming nonsense words. Maybe his mom shopped the way we did. Come to think of it, I might have been training my boys to someday write books read by thousands and thousands of children. I *might* have been, but in truth I didn't have that as a long-term goal. I wasn't thinking about giving my sons ideas for a future best seller; instead, I wanted them to find joy in whatever they were doing.

I took this on as my job. Being married to *Colonel* Smiley, a United States Air Force Reserve pilot, meant I was destined to handle the majority of fun in our home. I remember hearing him tell the boys with just a hint of teasing in his voice, "Be good to Mom. If anything ever happens to her there won't be any more fun around here." My line was always, "Every home needs an adult. Two might be overkill." In our home, Dad was happy to serve as the token adult, leaving me the role as chief fun-maker.

My husband, John, and our boys weren't the only ones who benefited from my commitment to joy and fun. We led a high school youth ministry for many years, which attracted a houseful of kids through the years. We live on a farm near a small community and our youth program managed to reach out to teenagers from many churches. One evening I actually counted and there were ten different churches represented. How was that possible? My role was to structure the fun to give the kids a closer look at biblical truths. I'd spend hours working on the lesson, hoping it would touch the heart of that young man who had been attending for only a few months, or that girl whose family was in turmoil. My goal was to have fun with a purpose, that purpose being to touch the lives of others and draw them to the kingdom. Joy is powerful and it's a wonderfully tasty fruit of the Spirit.

Opportunities continued to enter my life. I was asked to speak to group after group and was ultimately encouraged by a publishing house to write, in my own lighthearted way, about the choices that can be made to obtain peace and joy and sweet communion with Christ. I found many women hungry to experience joy and laughter and fun, eager to live free of the "if onlys and what ifs" that had been stifling their joy.

I am not joyful by any accident of nature. I grew up in a home that was anything but happy. Our family consisted of two older siblings who were both away at college by the time I was eight, my mother who was a homemaker, and my father, a dentist and (drumroll, please) a functional alcoholic. Mom grew up as a member of an affluent family in the suburbs of Chicago at a time when there was still an occasional farm between her home and the city. Dad grew up on a farm far from the city and far from affluence. His hard-fought degree in dentistry afforded him the ability to escape the life he had known, but it didn't protect him from the disease of alcoholism.

My mom and dad brought out the worst in one another. They had eloped when my mother was just out of high school and my dad was working as an apprentice in a dentist's office near Mom's home. This dashing young professional swept her off her feet and before anyone could give either of them wise counsel, they were married.

When our family embarked on a road trip, we didn't hear any version of my favorite words, "Come on, fun seekers! It's time to go!" It didn't matter where we were going, Mom and Dad were too close for comfort in an automobile. It began right in the driveway. My father would light his cigarette, adjust his rearview mirror, and fiddle with the radio all at the same time, while Mom, in a high-pitched scream, declared we were all headed for destruction if he didn't concentrate on his driving. Dad then turned the radio louder, stepping on the gas, hurling something equally unpleasant and demeaning to Mom. And off we went! No fun seekers in this car. I sat there trying to find my own internal happy place until the car stopped at my grandmother's home. Merry Christmas!

Although Mom and Dad never divorced, I seldom saw my mother living in joy. She was in her late fifties when Dad died. His death didn't change her attitude. She had practiced misery for so long, I suppose it was simply more comfortable to continue living that way. My mother's own words summarized her view of life's circumstances. "I did one foolish thing [married Dad] and I paid for it for the rest of my days." I wish she had chosen to be joyful in Christ in spite of her circumstances.

Mom was a glass-half-empty woman, to put it kindly. She was actually more of a get-that-glass-off-the-table-it's-going-to-leave-a-ring woman who had married a free-spirited guy with a drinking problem. All her adult life, Mom was on the lookout for a pending disaster and when Dad was still alive, he was usually willing and able to accommodate her.

I, on the other hand, see the glass as half full even if there is only a sip at the very bottom. I believe we all have the ability to choose our attitudes. The prescription for avoiding a negative one is to choose to read, believe, and live by the Word of God that imparts the attitude of Christ. It's a choice that's available to everyone. Consider Jesus's words: "I am the way and the truth and the life. No one comes to the Father except through me" (John 14:6). And, "You will know the truth, and the truth will set you free" (John 8:32).

Knowing the One who is the truth is the best place to start the journey to freedom. Jesus will help you see your circumstances in light of the truth and deal with them his way. For me that meant believing and embracing God's love for me and, in turn, loving him in return. The next step was beginning the process of forgiving my father and my mother and adjusting my attitude to reflect the joy of Jesus.

Mom was and will always be my inspiration. Until the day I die, no matter my circumstances, I want to speak and write and pray and live with the contagious joy of the Lord as my strength. As Nehemiah says, "Go and enjoy choice food and sweet drinks, and send some to those who have nothing prepared. This day is holy to our Lord. Do not grieve, for the joy of the LORD is your strength" (Nehemiah 8:10).

"Come on, fun seekers! It's time to go!"

Paula Huston

Paula is the author of two novels and seven works of spiritual nonfiction. Her most recent book is *One Ordinary Sunday: A Meditation on the Mystery of the Mass*. Paula is an oblate of a contemplative Catholic monastery. Paula and her husband, Mike, raise olives, fruit, vegetables, chickens, and bees on four acres on the central coast of California, where they have lived for the past thirty-three years. She divides her days between their four young grandchildren, their little farm, the monastery, and her writing.

The Good Earth

I am on the phone, staring out the window at the slashing rain, the wildly spinning windmill, when the first one goes over: an eighty-foot eucalyptus in a long line of them, planted over fifty years ago by our free-thinking neighbor as a wind break or a privacy screen or perhaps even a political statement of some kind. Over it goes in a tangle of power lines with an initial bounce off our fence and a hysterical flurry of leaves, and then the fence gives way beneath it.

Miraculously, it missed the chicken coop, though moments later, the coop roof goes spinning off in a seventy-mile-per-hour gust. I am still on the call when the second tree, then the third, go down. By the end of the hour, five will have fallen. Our power will be off for days. Nature, taking her course.

Yet in spite of that storm and those trees and the shock of them simply toppling like that—despite nature's power to stop me from walking or talking or putting two thoughts together if she so chooses—I make this vow: even if someone has to wheel me out the door or carry me like an infant or push my bed to the window and take off the screen and help me lay my face against the sill so I can feel the sun on my eyelids, I will always, every day, get myself outdoors till the moment there's no need anymore, thanks to the good black earth that will by then be cradling me.

For in the long run, it does not matter what the wind does; it is the great outdoors that ultimately sustains us, and this has always seemed a C. S. Lewis–type miracle to me. Perhaps the writer Pearl Buck was honoring this steadfast side of nature when she titled her most famous novel *The Good Earth*. Our home for the past thirty-three years has been in the middle of four fine acres on the central coast of California where, given our semiarid Mediterranean climate, we are able to grow or raise much of what we eat: vegetables, stone fruit, berries; olives for oil; grapes for wine; bees for honey; super-sweet greenhouse tomatoes for pure gustatory joy, even during the coldest part of winter. It does not matter whether I am starting seeds or weeding or picking green beans from the vines, I am always aware of being a wiser, calmer, more hopeful person when I am on my knees with my hands in the soil and the sun is washing the garden, bathing me in the warmth and splendor of its light.

The high mountains are another story; instead of comforting and sustaining me, they confront me with a hard truth: just how small I am in the midst of the vast universe. Backpacking above the tree line in the granite-gray Sierras confirms what I don't want to admit: we humans with all our sound and fury are like the alpine grasses that burst forth through snowmelt and vanish by fall. This trail we are on is hard, our time is short, we come and go before we can fully grasp what it means to be alive. These, at least, are the sorts of deep thoughts I have once I am back in civilization and nostalgically reliving the hike. But by the third day on the actual trail with life now down to pumping water, gathering wood, and bandaging my blisters, philosophy has given way to reality: I am nothing but a creature among creatures, a body whose animal needs demand all my focus and concentration. On the trail, my usually busy mind goes slack-jawed and opaque. I watch my boots and the dust that billows up beneath them. I look at the sky and wonder how hot it's going to be by noon. Should I slather on more sunscreen or dig out my long-sleeved shirt instead? I am humbled, chastened, filled with gratitude for the brief, beautiful miles I will walk during this time that has been given to me.

I get a third long view at New Camaldoli Hermitage in Big Sur where

I have made retreats for the past twenty-five years. My "cell," whether it be a trailer on the mountainside or a room in the guesthouse, always faces the sea. I move my chair to the garden and sit for hours as the sun tracks its way across the sky and disappears into a flaming horizon. As on the Sierra hikes, I find that in the wilderness of Big Sur I am unable to think with my usual intensity. Instead, I deliberately give way, letting the outdoors take me over like a vine weaving its silent way around the eaves of a roof or through a broken screen. In this state of being overrun by nature, I begin to lose myself in something larger. Without moving a foot, I have crossed an invisible line, one that usually prevents me from venturing too far into the mystery. For a few brief moments, I see what I normally can't see and get an inkling of what the old monks of the desert must have meant when they spoke of contemplation.

Some day in the not-so-distant future my earthly body will return to the soil. Thanks to that semiarid Mediterranean climate of ours, the sun will shine gently down upon my grave. But eventually a big Pacific storm, the kind that topples eucalyptus trees, will come surging in along the coastline. The wild winds will rise and birds will battle to stay aloft as the rains hammer down upon my resting place. Given enough spinning air and saturated soil, one of the giant cemetery oaks may go into its own death spiral, its roots tearing straight out of the ground on its way to kiss the earth. But much as I have loved nature, I will not be troubled at the sound of its dying. For by then, naked and bright-eyed as a newborn, I will have permanently crossed over that invisible line and taken up a new life altogether in God's most splendid garden, the homeland of our hope.

K. Martha Levitt

Martha is a high school and college teacher of English and creative writing. She has had essays published in *Inspired House* magazine; is creator and advisor of *Cellar Door*, a literary journal for young people; and is the author of a children's book on creation. She holds master's degrees in creative writing and educational leadership. Before entering the education field, she worked in news, public relations, and advertising. She lives in her native Connecticut where she practices calligraphy, grows food, tends chickens, and makes jam with blackberries that grow along stone walls.

Building a Stone Wall

Stone walls run along the hills and roads in old New England towns where I grew up, anchored to the landscape like oak trees, creating incontrovertible boundaries, separating farm from farm, house from road, field from river. Their presence, steadfast and indomitable, holds us New Englanders to our land.

New Englanders build everything—houses and children, friendships, vocations, dreams—the way they build walls: rock upon rock, year upon year, we fit together the pieces like glittering chunks of geography, placing them into the walls of our making. We expect our life creations to outlast us, to stand as monuments, reflecting back to us our experiences, reminding us that we have lived, giving us order and tradition and history and a future. Everything in this part of the world carries that kind of strength and immutability, rightness and permanence.

Halfway through life, no one expects a wall to fall, much less to completely vanish.

Now, standing at a counter in the courthouse, asking for the papers, sobbing, choking on my saliva, I could feel a wall heaving. It had been eroding for years, stone by stone. Now I was tearing down what was left with my own hands.

A girl with a tight blond ponytail and a mint-green sweater handed me the papers through a slot at the bottom of a glass window. She wanted to know if all the information was correct. She pointed to names. The maiden name. The married name. The date and place of the marriage. These names, his and mine, had been side by side for so many years, a matching set, on so many documents asserting the unity of our decisions to live together, buy houses, open bank accounts, create companies, join churches, travel, receive benefits, bring children into the world. Now the names were blurry. Everything was blurry.

I wiped the tears from the paper with my wrist, a desperate gesture to rub away the disappointment, the injustice, the loss, the bitterness. In their twenties, my sisters and friends had taken risks and married their college sweethearts. They had forged the lives of their imaginations and built families and houses. Theirs were still standing—weathered perhaps, but holding together—structurally undamaged by storms.

This is the great promise of Christianity, of godliness. *It will be well with you.* The righteous will enjoy the fruit of their hands. Birds will nest in the branches of the mustard tree that sprang from a tiny seed of faith. You will prosper. You will be a tree planted by rivers of water—alive, productive, beautiful.

I had accepted the gradual changes of life: moving between states, selling beloved homes, watching children receive diplomas, tying wreaths to the graves of my grandparents. Then the earth suddenly shifted; my marriage was breaking. I was flailing to gain balance. I expected fidelity. I expected the rewards of my labor. We were supposed to grow old together, watching birds from the window, working on our son's farm, welcoming friends to our table, driving around town in an old Buick. I expected that our faith would strengthen our purpose together in the world. Our sons and daughters would solidify it. Even if everything else goes wrong, those truths are supposed to keep the wall in place.

Hewn from a family of wall builders, I did not expect that any earthly force could permanently erode the days we worked together building the family homestead, the church, the business, the gardens, the years strung together with squealing and tears, with pain and music, with parents and friends, with boys chopping and staking wood for winter fires and wrestling in the kitchen, with girls playing hopscotch in the driveway and making fairylands under the boughs of low-hanging pines.

I did not expect the permanent structures to crumble. I am God's child. I did not expect him to abandon me in this way. Despite their faults, he always establishes his children on firm ground and defends them. He surrounds them with goodness. For the sake of his own reputation, he makes his people beautiful.

Yet now, after three decades of building, I was crying over the loss of my youth, fighting a hopeless embarrassment for myself and for God. I was certain he had mistaken me for someone else. The sins of someone else's father were visiting me and my children. All the rules had changed.

The girl with the tight blond ponytail could not look at my eyes. She kept glancing at me and pointing to the empty boxes where I was supposed to sign. This was her job, a routine where women were always asking for divorce papers, where they stood in lines just like this one, every day, screaming expletives into cell phones, rehearsing the crimes of their spouses to anyone who would listen. On normal days, this was not a sanctuary for the grieving. People like me rarely show up at places like this. Even a stranger could see that. Even a stranger could hear the wall fall. At first, the pen wouldn't write. She handed me another one. I signed the papers.

~

My last daughter left home in October in the dead of night. The darkness, the dry maple leaves scattered over the grass and flagstone walks, the smell of autumn and last night's fire still in our hair and clothes—this leaving was a summary of all the other leavings that had already taken place. The son I said goodbye to in a Boston high-rise overlooking the Charles River; the one I hugged at the airport, in his flannel shirt and backpack, before he headed west, forever; the daughter I left, uncertain and afraid in a brick dormitory on a Midwestern campus; the one I kissed on the forehead, a little blond statue in a green dress, tiny and courageous against New York's skyscrapers and subway stairs and bumper-to-bumper yellow taxis.

This morning carried the weight of all those goodbyes. This daughter was going to California, where all twenty-three-year-olds go to find work and adventure and the essential piece of their soul that carries their destiny. We hugged and held hands, hugged and held hands. There was frenetic waving from the car windows and kiss-blowing and tossing of "I love you" back and forth. Then the taillights of the green jeep squiggled away, like red jelly, a long way down the country road, floating on the dark October air.

I had feared this moment, this final departure that would leave me without tangible realities to anchor me to soil and memory and place. Soon the house would be sold. Without the marriage, with the children now out in the world, all my reference points had shifted or disappeared.

Standing there alone, with clasped hands, yearning, mouthing prayers, I watched the taillights return. Backing in the same squiggly path, the Jeep came back. My daughter had one last thing to say. "I know it's cliché, and a poet already said it," she said, "but I want you to know, '*I carry you, I carry you in my heart.*'"

Like Mary, treasuring in her heart the incandescent joy and wonder of her Son, savoring in memory what she couldn't understand, my daughter's words lodged in me. They brought back something solid, a reality more substantial even than a stone wall. They shed light on the great Christian truth that every tangible, visible beauty, every life holds within it a mysterious piece of a greater reality. The life we build is not essentially in the houses and farms or the careers and products of our hands. The life we build is implanted within us. We carry its truths like nourishment, like life-giving water. This is the promise and mystery of all of the Scriptures—God, always before his people, beside them, and behind them, until he finally walks among them and lives within them. This heart-carrying, this sheltering, has always been the way to make a place of permanence, to create home.

With her leaving, my daughter was taking a reality, like a piece of permanent landscape, into her being, to remember and ponder, to wrap herself in and protect her along the way. "I carry you, too," I said. And then she drove away.

In that moment, I felt that I was breathing in grace. While all my work of all my years seemed to have vanished, I could still feel her skin against mine, her voice in the air. I breathed back into myself the grace of all those years, the truths that built us, the days we all lived together, the faith we held, the pain we inflicted and forgave, the prayers we taught and whispered and wrestled through, the hope we fed like a starving bird, the love we kept alive.

Madeleine L'Engle

Madeleine (1918–2007) did not begin publishing until after age forty. On her fortieth birthday, after receiving yet another rejection letter, she determined to give up on writing. Thankfully she didn't. She went on to write more than forty books, including the Newbery Medal–winning *A Wrinkle in Time* and its sequels: *A Wind in the Door*, National Book Award–winning *A Swiftly Tilting Planet*, *Many Waters*, and *An Acceptable Time*. In addition, Madeleine wrote many nonfiction works, including *Crosswicks Journals* and other explorations on the subjects of faith and art.

The Flesh Is to Be Honored

There is no more beautiful witness to the mystery of the word made flesh than a baby's naked body. I remember with sensory clarity sitting with one of my babies on my lap and running my hand over the incredibly pure smoothness of the bare back and thinking that any mother, holding her child thus, must have at least an echo of what it is like to be Mary; that in touching the particular created matter, flesh, of our child, we are touching the Incarnation. My son-in-law Alan, holding his daughter on his lap, running his hand over her bare back with the same tactile appreciation with which I had touched my children, made a similar remark.

Once, when I was in the hospital, the smooth and beautiful white back of the woman in the bed next to mine, a young woman dying of cancer, was a stabbing and bitter reminder of the ultimate end of all matter.

But not just our human bodies: all matter: the stars in their courses: everything: the end of time.

Meanwhile we are in time, and the flesh is to be honored. At all ages. For me, this summer, this has been made clear in a threefold way: I have fed, bathed, played pat-a-cake with my grandbabies. In the night when I wake up, as I usually do, I always reach out with a foot, a hand, to touch my husband's body; I go back to sleep with my hand on his warm flesh. And my mother is almost ninety and preparing to move into a different country. I do not understand the mysteries of the flesh, but I know that we must not be afraid to reach out to each other, to hold hands, to touch.

In our bedroom there is a large old rocking chair which was in the attic of Crosswicks when we bought it. It seems to have been made especially for mothers and babies. I have sat in it and nursed my babe in the middle of the night. I have sung innumerable lullabies from it. When Hugh was in *Medea*, which was sent overseas in 1951 by the State Department, I sat in the rocking chair, carrying his child within me and holding our firstborn in my arms, singing all the old lullabies, but especially "Sweet and Low" because of *over the Western sea* and *bring him again to me.*

This summer I sit in the rocking chair and rock and sing with one or other of my granddaughters. I sing the same songs I sang all those years ago. It feels utterly right. Natural. The same.

But it isn't the same. I may be holding a baby just as I used to hold a baby, but chronology has done many things in the intervening years, to the world, to our country, to my children, to me. I may feel, rocking a small, loving body, no older than I felt rocking that body's mother. But I am older bodily; my energy span is not as long as it used to be; at night my limbs ache with fatigue; my eyes are even older than the rest of me. It is going to seem very early—it is going to *be* very early—when the babies wake up: Alan, Josephine, Cynthia, and I take turns getting up and going downstairs with them, giving them breakfast, making the coffee. Is it my turn again so quickly?

Chronology: the word about the measurable passage of time, although its duration varies: How long is a toothache? How long is standing in line at the supermarket? How long is a tramp through the fields with the dogs or dinner with friends, or a sunset, or the birth of a baby?

Chronology, the time which changes things, makes them grow older, wears them out, and manages to dispose of them, chronologically, forever.

Thank God there is kairos, too: again the Greeks were wiser than we are. They had two words for time: *chronos* and *kairos*.

Kairos is not measurable. Kairos is ontological. In kairos we *are*, we are fully in isness, not negatively, as Sartre saw the isness of the oak tree, but fully, wholly, positively. Kairos can sometimes enter, penetrate, break through chronos: the child at play, the painter at his easel, Serkin playing the *Appassionata,* are in kairos. The saint at prayer, friends around the dinner table, the mother reaching out her arms for her newborn baby, are in kairos. The bush, the burning bush, is in kairos, not any burning bush, but the very particular burning bush before which Moses removed his shoes; the bush I pass on my way to the brook. In kairos that part of us which is not consumed in the burning is wholly awake. We too often let it fall asleep, not as the baby in my arms droops into sleepiness, but dully, bluntingly.

I sit in the rocking chair with a baby in my arms, and I am in both kairos and chronos. In chronos I may be nothing more than some cybernetic salad on the bottom left-hand corner of a check; or my social security number; or my passport number. In kairos I am known by name: Madeleine.

Gina Ochsner

Gina lives in Keizer, Oregon, and teaches writing and literature at Corban University and in Seattle Pacific's low-residency MFA program. She is the author of *The Necessary Grace to Fall*, which won the Flannery O'Connor Award, and *People I Wanted to Be*. Both short-story collections received the Oregon Book Award. Her novels are *The Russian Dreambook of Color and Flight* and *The Hidden Letters of Velta B*. To learn more, visit ginaochsner.com.

A Pilgrim in Progress

Medjugorje, the town where I'm headed, appears as a small dot on the map of eastern Bosnia-Herzogovina. I struggle to pronounce the name. *Medju* in Croatian and Serbian means between. *Gorje* means mountains. To get there I travel by train from Sarajevo, the capital of Bosnia, through the Neretva Valley. The dark river cuts through the jagged limestone mountains, like wire through cheese, hewing a path through massive stone outcroppings, some of which hang precariously over the water. Others protrude from the mountainside, looking as if enormous stone fists from within the mountain had tried to punch through.

Fog hovers in the dark valleys, hangs over the water, rises and falls as if it were breathing. I'm entering a world of tremendous beauty and heartache, a haunted world bearing wounds. The crumbled remains of bombed houses and barns dot the hillsides, a grim reminder of the war in 1992 in which so many lost their lives. But atrocity, I read in my travel guide, is nothing new in this part of the country.

In 1941, the Ustashe, a Croatian ultranationalist group, rounded up Serbian monks from a nearby monastery and threw them into pits not far from Medjugorje. A few months later, thirteen hundred Serbian civilians were, like the monks, thrown into pits and left to die. Forty years later, against this backdrop of violence, six teenagers living in

Medjugorje saw Mary. These sightings would no doubt have been dismissed as a hoax, or the collective hallucination of suggestible teenagers, had not Mary continued to visit these mystics, now in their early fifties, over a period of many years.

Since the first sightings, over thirty million people have journeyed to Medjugorje, about one million each year. My reason for traveling three thousand miles to this remote pilgrimage site is, by my own estimation, ambiguous. I could say I am a pilgrim by proxy. A good friend of mine had for many years wanted to come. For a variety of reasons, she couldn't, and I could. But as I walk from the tiny bus station toward the Catholic church where throngs of pilgrims cluster beside the outdoor stalls, I know I don't belong here.

Raised a Presbyterian, I learned to love the quiet, somber God of the Presbyterians. That God crept silently from one stained glass pane to another, casting long swaths of colored light in the air, over the pews, the clean floor, our shoulders. After ten years at that church, our family left and joined a Pentecostal assembly. I loved and feared the God of the Pentecostals. This God rushed like wind, alighted as fire, visited people in dreams, and delivered prophetic messages.

Some years later, I put the Pentecostal Assembly behind me and went to graduate writing school. But as I passed the Catholic church on my way to classes each day, I thought of my friend. I remembered her fierce intellectual and spiritual enquiry and how it led her to Catholicism. I remembered her devotion and how for her, the church was a sanctuary and refuge. At that point in my life, I needed a refuge. I was in an abusive relationship and I was not thriving in graduate school. Rather than buckle down and prove to the program director how serious I was about writing, I took a job at a cheese and puppet shop and enrolled in Russian language classes. I attended martial arts classes to help me get the courage to ditch my fiancé, and I joined the Roman Catholic initiation class at St. Thomas Aquinas Catholic Church.

The little parish of St. Thomas Aquinas became the oasis in my spiritual desert, a burning coal in the deep midwinter of my heart. I loved old white-haired Father Dismus and how he skipped down the aisle to the altar. I loved the other parishioners and the pursuit of the holy amidst the profane and ordinary. I loved their deep generosity. And then, as I so often did, I left.

~

Special tour buses convey pilgrims to Medjugorje from all parts of Europe and beyond. No pilgrim, it seems, journeys for precisely the same reason. Some are here to see a sign. Some are veteran pilgrims; they have spent and will spend the rest of their lives visiting holy sites. Some are seeking a spiritual cleansing and are willing to stand in long lines outside the row of confessionals for their turn in a stall. Some are in desperate need of healing; their afflictions are obvious; their crutches and wheelchairs are obediently parked nearby. I skirt the confessionals. Four are designated for those wishing to confess to a Croatian priest, four for those wanting a Serbian priest. None are set aside for English speakers. I sigh in relief and head for the stations of the cross trail.

A placard at the trailhead depicts an ice-cream cone, a camera, a phone, and a book. A thick white slash cuts through each. No eating, no photography, no talking, and apparently, no reading. "No problem," I mutter as a Swedish couple with alpine walking sticks breeze past me. They notice my flimsy shoes. My camera hanging from my neck. My notepad clutched in one hand. They don't know about the power bar melting in my pocket which I fully intend to eat anyway. Amateur, their gazes imply. Or worse, imposter.

Tall and wide and set on end like enormous coins, the stations are made of gray limestone. Each station has a scene carved in bas-relief and each is placed about three hundred yards from each other, con-nected by steep switchbacks and treacherous inclines. My many years of treadmilling has in no way prepared me for this. The sharp rocks puncture the thin soles of my shoes. I'm questioning this hike. I'm ques-tioning my motives.

As I reach station seven near the top of the trail I am arrested mid step. A man in what looks to be a very expensive suit has flung himself against the station. He hugs the stone, kisses the carved image of a suf-fering Christ. His shoulders shake and I can't tell if he's sobbing or in ecstasy, but it's a moment of such spiritual ardor, such naked devotion, I can't look away. My cheeks burning, I tiptoe past him, shamed by his passion.

As I'm sliding on my butt down a steep wash of rock, it occurs to me that at some point along my spiritual journey I had once had the same kind of fiery passion that radiated from the man at station seven. And now I don't. Now I am very uncomfortable and not just because of the razor-sharp rocks slicing my backside. The gospel is wildly disruptive, extravagantly revolutionary. How had I forgotten that? When and why did I become a spiritual surfer, sampling Christianity as if it were a large buffet from which I could pick and choose what pleased me, piling high my plate with what I liked, turning my nose up at what I didn't? How did I become a voyeur, content to watch other people in transformation, applauding their growth and their discovery, unwilling to ask why it wasn't happening to me?

<hr/>

At the base of Apparition Hill, Mary is everywhere: Mary in the shops, Mary on printed cards, Mary fashioned as small figurines designed to sit on end tables or desktops. Phalanxes of larger statues meant for hallways or yards line the sidewalks. Stickers of Mary, serene with her eyes downcast, grace bottles of wine and rose-scented perfume. A bottle of Mary wine in my backpack, I begin the climb up Apparition Hill where I hear the rosary chanted and sung in Italian, Croatian, even Japanese. Small groups have staked out their spots at the top of the hill, their gear spread out in front of an enormous marble white statue of Mary.

It's 5:50. Mary, if she's going to show, is supposed to make her appearance in about twenty minutes. Some, I read in my travel guide, don't actually see Mary, but instead observe their rosaries changing color, or the sun spinning.

At 6:00 a number of people move closer to the statue and kneel. I keep my gaze on the sky. The air is thick and brooding. Oily clouds stretch the sky and behind them a cataract sun burns like a blind white eye.

At 6:08 I feel something bubbling inside me. I choose to call it hope. I believe in miracles. I have witnessed many, have been the recipient of a few. At 6:10 I stare at the sun. Nothing. At 6:11 I squint at the other pilgrims. They are praying, chanting, singing. They are not looking at their watches. I return my gaze to the greasy sky. And I wait. And I wait. I can't look at the sun without seeing spots and feeling the pop and buzz at the base of my neck that signals an impending migraine. But I am strangely content. I am absurdly happy sitting on these sharp rocks and doing absolutely nothing.

I remember a story I read in *Buber's Tales of the Hassidim*. A young devout Jew rushes to and fro, maintaining a blistering pace throughout his day. But he is profoundly dissatisfied. He meets with his rabbi. "Rabbi," he says, "I pray, I fast. I do all that the law says. I do this to the best of my ability and with all my heart. Why is God so far away from me?"

The rabbi studies the young man carefully, then says, "Stand still and let God catch up to you."

That night, as I lay on the little bed in the hostel Gloria, darkness folds around me. I think about my own strange journeys, so many of them undertaken without purpose or plans. This one was no different. I had no contacts in Bosnia-Herzogovina. I had no language skills. I was traveling alone and had come here on a whim. I had come in search of a sign or a miracle. And in spite of my lack of spiritual preparation, I had been given one.

~

"What is the meaning of life? What is the answer? Tell me!" a man demanded at a recent reading. I looked longingly at the exit. Two elderly women in fold-out chairs leaned forward slightly. I was trapped.

"Well, it's the pursuit of truth," I murmured.

"Well, have you found it?" His tone was combative and in a different context I might have laid all my cards out on the table, recited the Nicene Creed, told him the reason why I even breathe or want to keep breathing is because of Jesus. But I've learned to be cautious at public libraries. I deployed another smile that unfolded like a mechanical umbrella.

"Tell me!" he insisted.

"In the research and travels I've done I've been asking people that very same question. I think it's at the heart of being human. We are designed with a desire to have purpose and find meaning," I said, my gaze again locking on the exit door. "Stories are a powerful way of organizing the chaos of our world. I'm trying to find and tell stories that work like maps guiding us toward something worth finding."

He snorted, hardly able to contain his bile. Not to be put off, after the reading he cornered me by the coffee and cookie table. "It seems to me that you have spent a fair number of years and energy searching and questing for something. I just hope you find it," he said.

Driving home in the dark, the windshield wipers swishing and squeaking, I thought of Medjugorje. I remembered the man at station seven. I remembered the quiet calm that broke open inside of me as I sat under a wobbling sky and gazed at the sun. I had found what I was looking for and it had found me. But in finding it, I must keep up the search. This is not to say that God has hidden himself from me. During my younger years of utter misery and sorrow, much of it of my own making, God was, like light through stained-glass windows, casting color and shape in the air all about me. But with my gaze collapsed inward, I didn't see it. And while I wandered from faith, pouring water on my fire, God breathed over the coals with a patience that can only be called unconditional love. And now, just shy of fifty, it's my turn to breathe over the coals. This is to say I am often uncomfortable, as, I think, I should be. I am seeking. I am finding God, again and again, daily, hourly.

I did not expect time to work this way in me. I thought as I approached fifty, I would grow content in my understanding of who God is and who I am meant to be; I thought I would grow content to sit. I thought as I grew older I would want to walk less, explore less, settle down. But the opposite has happened. I don't know where these rocky paths will lead as I press onward. It's not a smooth commute, this sojourn. The rocks will puncture my soles. I will stumble, and I will fall. And I will thank God every day for it. An amateur, an imposter—maybe. But mostly, still a pilgrim.

Jen Pollock Michel

Jen is a writer and speaker who lives with her husband and five children in Toronto. She is the author of *Teach Us to Want: Longing, Ambition, and the Life of Faith,* Christianity Today's 2015 Book of the Year. Jen also writes for *Today in the Word* and is a regular contributor to Christianity Today's *Her.meneutics* and *Gifted for Leadership* blogs. She earned her BA in French from Wheaton College and her MA in literature from Northwestern University. You can find Jen at her nearest farmer's market or at jenpollockmichel.com.

This Is Forty

For our fortieth birthdays, my husband and I threw a lavish party for one another. The next morning, I stood in the shower, heaving unexpected sobs. I wasn't unhappy. My best friend had flown in for the occasion, and on the day of the party, we had strung lights on the deck, bought extra wine glasses, and gotten pedicures—an impromptu indulgence necessitating a giggly purchase of two-dollar flip-flops at a corner convenience store. The evening of the party, the doorbell began ringing while the caterers bustled in the kitchen, and the servers circulated with wine. A large crowd of family and friends gathered, and my husband and I had delivered ringing toasts to one another. *To the man I've most admired. To my wife and her first book.* It was a night for celebrating that life ran sweet with goodness.

Why then the wracking sobs the morning after? Because when life struck forty, I appreciated, in some new way, that life's goodness was episodic and fitful. That it was all going so quickly, and I couldn't save any of it. To be human, living post–Genesis 3, is to suffer life's fragility. There is nothing *forever* about twenty-one or forty-one or eighty-one. Time indeed runs out.

In Marilynne Robinson's novel *Gilead,* John Ames, nearly seventy and terminally ill, writes to his seven-year-old son a testament of his life. He tells his son that in his tenure as pastor of a small rural church, he had often been tasked with consoling the dying—of assuring them, when they asked, that death was like "going home." Nevertheless, on the eve of his own death, Ames can't help wishing for more time himself. "I want your dear perishable self," he writes to his young son, "to live long and to love this poor perishable world, which I somehow cannot imagine not missing bitterly."

At seventy, standing on the threshold between this world and the next, John Ames is a likely candidate to be brooding on death. At forty, I am not. Yet at the same time, my own father died before he grayed— he, forty-something, I, eighteen, and lacking keen sense of the injustice. When friends and family gathered all those years ago, lining up to convey their condolences for this *young* man's death, it made so little sense to me at the time. But now that I am heading into midlife, I feel my own entitlement to more decades. *I wish to borrow more time.*

How do I die? And die well? We aren't as preoccupied with these questions as perhaps we should be, especially because the Bible itself insists that life can only be lived well with mortality in view. "Our days may come to seventy years, or eighty, if our strength endures; . . . for they quickly pass, and we fly away. . . . Teach us to number our days, that we may gain a heart of wisdom" (Psalm 90:10, 12). I picture Moses praying these words, so much lived faith behind him: his youngest years as a son of Pharaoh, 40 years of Egyptian exile, 40 more years of wilderness wandering, 120 years in all. Even Moses, at the time of his death, felt himself young. As the Bible records, "His eyes were not weak nor his strength gone" (Deuteronomy 34:7). But Moses knew there could be no forever. There was only ever today.

To think of death is to properly appraise time, and brooding on life's end has the unsung benefits of helping us to live purposefully. The writer of Ecclesiastes follows his philosophical musings on the meaning of work and wealth and ambition to their logical terminus: to death, when "the days of trouble come and the years approach when you will say, 'I find no pleasure in them'" (12:1). This ancient king, who had achieved for himself a vast array of pleasures, wanted us to understand something of today's temporality. Like the sun, our lives will dip below the horizon line of time. Day will turn to night, and to envision this extinguishing is to grasp for eternity's light. See yourselves old, he implores. He notes that if, by God's providence, we end our days in old age, with bodies frail and stooped, we will come finally to grieve our wasted time of chasing "vanity of vanities." Our ambitions, like our vision, will have dimmed. Our haste after achievement, like our gait, will have slowed. We will wonder at the futility of all the mistaken hurry.

The greatest of life's tragedies will be the delinquent resolution to live and love well, and regret will be the payment we exact, in Augustine's words, for the "immoderate urge towards those things which are at the bottom end of the scale of good, [having] abandon[ed] the higher and supreme goods, that is you, Lord God, and your truth and your law."[1] On the eve of death, we will all wish we had loved rightly. And worshipped well.

"There is actually no such thing as atheism," said David Foster Wallace. "There is no such thing as not worshipping. Everybody worships. The only choice we get is what to worship."[2] Wallace, who ended his own life despite his achieved and forecasted literary success, may have understood something about "vanity."

I read these Scriptures I've referenced in new ways now—at forty— and take into this next decade a sobered appraisal of time and a more determined desire for purpose. For me, that means slowing down for the act of presence. For the time that is left, I want to be happier to be less historic. I have fewer grand plans; I only want to be more ambitious for greater love. Achievement that keeps no company effects a terrible loneliness.

And still, I want to keep writing. There's marvel for me in the ancient prophecy given to Joel. "Your sons and daughters will prophesy. . . . Even on my servants, both men and women, I will pour out my Spirit in those days" (Joel 2:28–29). I want to take my place in those words, and as opportunity is granted me, be a living voice for the proclamation of this good news: that in Jesus, death is not final, and we are *going home.*

I don't know what God has planned for my second act: whether my lifespan will be twice that of my father's, or whether I, too, will die young.

But I know this: I must protest what Pastor Greg Thompson has called, the "original demonic lie": *You shall not surely die.*

Thoughts of death accompanied me to worship recently, and not coincidentally, our text was Acts 7. The scene is the death of Stephen, a young man so full of promise. But before drawing his final breath, Stephen sees "the heavens opened, and the Son of Man standing at the right hand of God" (v. 56). Our pastor noted that in his commentary on Acts, F. F. Bruce makes this case: that at the moment Stephen confesses Jesus to the crowds, Jesus confesses Stephen to the Father. The Son of God receives Stephen home.

If only for this grace for whatever time remains. To be faithful and fearless—and finally, eternally, fall into the arms of Jesus.

I think I could go like that.

Notes

1. Augustine, *The Confessions* 2.v.10.
2. David Foster Wallace, commencement address, May 21, 2005, Kenyon College, Ohio, transcript, https://web.ics.purdue.edu/~drkelly/DFWKen yonAddress2005.pdf.

Jill Kandel

Jill grew up in North Dakota, riding her Appaloosa bareback across the prairie. She married a man from the Netherlands and worked overseas for ten years in Zambia, Indonesia, England, and the Netherlands. Kandel's first book, *So Many Africas: Six Years in a Zambian Village*, won the Autumn House Nonfiction Prize and the Sarton Women's Literary Award. Her essays have appeared in *Best Spiritual Writing 2012* and in *The Magic of Memoir*. She blogs about writing life and living between cultures at her website, jillkandel.com.

Naked I Came

When I was younger I never thought about being old. Young life, like young love, is a blind thing. There are so many things that do not cross your mind when you are at the beginnings of your life. I never thought of limitations, marrying a foreigner, civil wars, Lyme disease, miscarriages, or an aging body. When I was young, life was unfilled and waiting. Lately, since I've passed the sixty mark, I've begun to consider things that were once completely off my radar. My home-going. My own death. The legacy I will leave behind.

Perhaps, these thoughts would have been too morbid as a teenager. But now—though they sometimes strike me as unnatural—they are actually, rather surprisingly, appropriate. They are necessary.

My husband and I have lost all four of our parents now. We are the next elderly.

When I think of my dad, I remember the stories he told of his doctoring. The accidents: train wrecks, motorcycles wrapped up in barbed wire fences, a rodeo clown gored by a bull. I remember the near misses: a farmer caught neck-deep in a grain bin, the little boy pulled nearly too late from the swimming pool bottom, the man with a sore jaw rushed to the nearest large hospital, a heart attack in the making. I remember the patients my dad helped to pull through. I remember the stories of the ones he lost. "I brought that boy into the world," he told me once, "and I saw him out. Only twenty-one years old. Cancer. His mother and I were the ones with him at his birth, and we were with him again, at his end."

I miss my father. I miss his laughter, his quiet kindness, his keen intelligence. It's easy to remember his face, his lanky frame, the confidence he portrayed, the nonchalant way he strode through life. Sometimes, I see him in my son.

When I think of my mother, I am more muddled—her life strung and tangled throughout my life in complicated knots. I could tell you a thousand things too many about my mother. Her need for pheasant-feathered hats and purple suede shoes, her wacky sense of humor, her facelifts, her institutionalizations, her love of storytelling. She—North Dakota Republican Woman of the Year—attended Nixon's inaugural ball wearing an orange chiffon empress dress and long white dancing gloves. My mother lived a life vibrant to the point of tears, both hers and mine. Happy! How my mother could laugh. Weeping. How she handed me her tears to hold, and I dried them with my own.

My Dutch mother-in-law, Jopie, is a blur in my mind. A hazy, friendly, sweet mirage. When I step close to peer at her, she disappears into the fog of Dutch/English language miscommunications. For most of our life, we lived continents apart. I barely knew her. By the time I learned to speak Dutch, she was already lost in her own world of Alzheimer's. I wish I had known her better. I liked her very much.

When I think of my Dutch father-in-law, Izaak, I cannot help but think of the choice he made at the end of his life. Euthanasia. 2008. Legal in the Netherlands. Suffice it to say that on the day he died he was eighty-five years old; he still cooked his own meals; he still drove his own car, still went to museums, to concerts, to the library. He had dozens of friends. He was a pastor.

Izaak's life and death walk hand in hand in my mind. I do not know how to separate the two. I do not know how to read a book and separate it from its ending. His life is something like that, like a book with an ending that dissatisfies. A book I want to throw across the room; I want to rewrite the ending.

When my parents died, they left behind an estate brimming full with antiques, collectables, first edition books, Tiffany lamps. They are mostly things that people no longer want. My mother, an antique dealer, always said, "This is my legacy to you. Your inheritance."

Sorry, Mom. It's turned out to be a burden. Check the web. Antiques are everywhere. Her generation of collectors is dying off. My generation is getting older and downsizing. And my children? The last thing they want is Grandma's old chair, even if it's remarkably historic. They have no time for Fenton glassware or Westmoreland Milk Glass. They turn their noses up at Fire King, Heisey, or Imperial Glass. The market's glutted. Even eBay is a bust. We have forty-five boxes of antiques nobody knows what to do with. Too *valuable* to give away, yet no one really wants them.

My husband and I have said, "We will not do this to our children." Part of aging well, for us, is cleaning up the house, sorting, organizing, throwing. This is a gift I can give my children now, that in ten or twenty years will be beyond me.

But there is another gift. A harder one. That we need to consider. It is not just the heirlooms we own and pass down physically that matter. There is one more legacy to consider.

When I was in the Netherlands last year, my sister-in-law arranged for us to meet a local author who writes about death and dying. The author had spent three years interviewing people, asking them about deathbed experiences. She interviewed people in the medical profession: doctors, nurses, hospice workers. She interviewed people of faith: Buddhist monks, Christian clergy, Muslim clerics. She talked to people who have been with loved ones when they died.

We had tea and talked about death and dying. We discussed euthanasia and palliative care in the Netherlands. I asked the author, "In three years of interviewing people and talking about death, what is the most important thing you've learned?"

She thought a long time. Sipped her tea. Then softly said, "You have to be naked."

"What do you mean?" I asked, confused, wondering if she was speaking literally.

"To have a good death, you have to be willing to not hide yourself. To be vulnerable and open. Our suffering has a purpose; it helps us let go; it helps us soften and give ourselves away. Death humbles us."

We talked a long time. "Life is precious," she said. "Death is precious, too."

On the way back home, my sister-in-law and I couldn't stop talking. She needed that meeting as much as I did. It had been nine years, but she was still trying to put together the threads of her father's death.

That evening, I thought long and hard about our conversations. I was reminded of the words of Job: "Naked I came from my mother's womb, and naked shall I return" (Job 1:21 ESV).

⁓

The word *palliative* comes from the medieval Latin *palliativus*, meaning *under cloak*. A covering. A protection. A shield. There is a hint of the covert within the word. A concealing.

In today's vocabulary, palliative refers to medical care that alleviates symptoms or problems without addressing underlying causes. Palliative care shields the body from itself, covers, protects the dying from their own frame.

I think about this word. About the ways we shield and cover ourselves. I think about the words *naked* and *vulnerable*, which leads me to crustaceans, the lobsters and crabs and shrimp that carry their skeletons externally.

In order to grow, crustaceans must molt, shed those external hard shells, those carapaces, or they die, trapped within their own outer skeletons. This process of molting is a place of great vulnerability for the creature, a dangerous place with little protection.

When a grasshopper molts, it leaves a perfect replica of itself behind, the exuvia. A shell so delicate you can see through it. A transparent likeness.

I think of my father-in-law. Trapped within his own skin, trapped within the protections and fears and shells he built around himself. His inability to shed control. Without the shed, there is no growth. Without vulnerability, the rigidity of our protective shell becomes its own death sentence. Shed the outer skin. Or die.

The process of dying is our last molt. Death our final carapace.

We want everything so quick, so orderly, so efficient. Sterile and controlled. The very thing we are afraid of is that which sets us free. We must stand naked and vulnerable before death. We must be humble. We must let it have its way, not rip the shell away.

Even nature teaches so.

I am not afraid to die; I am afraid to die. While simultaneously trying to hold both of these oxymoronic statements together, I also acknowledge this, my firm belief: God holds the breath of life; it is his to hold not mine.

The choices we will make in death will affect the living, the left behind. Like it or not, we—the modern elderly—are living with a growing array of choices. They are complicated beyond belief. How are we going to deal with the sheer unholy number of choices that we face?

Although there are no easy answers, our decisions matter gravely. The choices we make will affect the next generation, and the next. They will not go away.

And this, our ending place, is perhaps the most courageous place of all. Facing it. Praying it. Thinking it. Talking it. Clearly and unflinchingly. As an aging woman, I want to do this last thing well. In believing. And in hope. I want to always choose to trust God.

I want to believe in this: God knows what he is doing.

And as we transition into that place where it is said, "There will be no more death or mourning or crying or pain," may we honor God, to our final breath.

EPILOGUE: THE BOOK OF WONDERING

I stood at the edge of the grave, wind whipping my hair. Forty of us, clutching our coats, stood in clusters in the grassy hillocks, the ocean foaming behind us. We tried to sing against the wind "Be Thou My Vision" and "Amazing Grace." Each of the three sons spoke in turn. We glanced at each other, then at the casket in front of us, suspended over the grave on spruce planks. Then it was my turn. I gripped the piece of paper tighter and pitched my voice above the wind, reading these well-known words from Ecclesiastes:

> There is a time for everything,
>   and a season for every activity under the heavens:
>
> a time to be born and a time to die,
> a time to plant and a time to uproot,
> a time to kill and a time to heal,
> a time to tear down and a time to build,
> a time to weep and a time to laugh,
> a time to mourn and a time to dance,
> a time to scatter stones and a time to gather them.
>
> (3:1–5)

Everyone traveled by boat to our tiny Alaskan island, braving an icy wind and ocean waves—arriving wet and shivering. They were all commercial salmon fishermen, like us. After the reading and the prayer, we walked slowly on the trail the backhoe had made to the back side of the island, where the grave had been dug. We lowered the casket tied with fisherman's knots into the hole and dropped a shovelful or a handful of dirt.

Above the casket, the sun was as bright as I'd ever seen it. It looked as though the skin of the world had been peeled back to its viscera: the grasses, the wind, the ocean foaming white and blue at our backs, everything noisily throbbing and pulsing with life. How could a burial be so beautiful?

The week before the service, when my husband asked if I wanted to read a Bible passage, I knew what I would read. Ecclesiastes has long been one of my favorite books. The book misbehaves. The writer, called "the Preacher," asks hard questions. He sounds anything but holy, opening with a phrase that sounds like a teenager high on cynicism, or the lyrics from an existential rock song, "Meaningless! Meaningless! . . . Everything is meaningless." The phrase keeps appearing like a ghost in and out of a leaning house.

The first chapter reads like a sigh and a moan:

> What do people gain from all their labors
>   at which they toil under the sun?
> Generations come and generations go,
>   but the earth remains forever.
> The sun rises and the sun sets,
>   and hurries back to where it rises.
> The wind blows to the south
>   and turns to the north;
> round and round it goes,
>   ever returning on its course.
>   (vv. 3–6)

From there the Preacher wanders and circles through most of life's paradoxes and confusions. The book presents no argument. It's messy and even contradictory at times. It's brutally honest.

> Everyone comes naked from their mother's womb,
>   and as everyone comes, so they depart.
> They take nothing from their toil
>   that they can carry in their hands.
>   (5:15)

Some commentators and readers over the centuries have insisted this "wisdom book" could not be canonical, could not be inspired by God. Where is the cheer, the victory, the triumph of the Christian life?

The hearts of people, moreover, are full of evil and there is madness in their hearts while they live, and afterward they join the dead. (9:3)

No one is spared. Even writers get a dose of reality:

> The more the words,
> the less the meaning,
> and how does that profit anyone?
> (6:11)

In every exploration, the Preacher circles back to the hardest question, the question we often don't ask until we're forty or fifty; the question we've all been asking in every essay here: As the sun rises and sets from decade to decade, what is it all for? What is it good for us to do all our days under the sun?

When I turned forty, I went for a walk on the loop of our gravel road with my husband and our four kids. It was November. The kids dragged sticks in the road and chased each other; I kicked the sparse alder leaves fallen to the road's edge and thought about getting old. About what kind of old woman I wanted to be. I had just started to color my hair, which was graying around my face. I didn't want to be invisible. I didn't want to blanche into pale translucence and fade away with a whisper. I was already making plans. When I was eighty, I would go shopping in a purple jogging suit. I would wear bright red lipstick until I died. I would be kind. Generous. I would stay interesting. I wouldn't atrophy into a daily round of doctor appointments, my sphere of mind and spirit and speech shrinking to the functions of my body. I didn't want to get old. Somehow, my body mistook this cue, and at forty-three I was pregnant. And nearly two years later, unexpectedly, another baby. At forty-five, back to the beginning again. It was a time to mourn. And a time to be born. Now I could not grow old.

When I turned fifty, I woke up that morning with an eye infection and my husband threw me a party. A houseful of friends came for lunch. The night before, my mother and sister had jumped out of a closet, flying all the way from the East Coast to surprise me. We ate huge cold-cut sandwiches and cheesecake, drank root beer and lemonade, and laughed. I asked everyone to bring a recipe or a story. We spoke around the table, one by one.

Sue, ten years older than I am, gave me the best present of all: "I loved my fifties. It was the best decade ever," she said, smiling at me.

Then the sun rose and set, the rivers drained into the ocean, my kids grew. My mothers and fathers died. I scattered stones. I mourned. I wondered how to live with such losses.

Now I am turning sixty. I am not old yet, but I am closer than I was. I have a daughter who's a professor. I have a married son and two teenagers. I spend days locked in closets wrestling with God, writing books. I travel. I teach. I pluck the gray from my eyebrows. I try to hide my wrinkles. I grieve the thickening of my waist. I am happy to be alive. I wear bright lipstick every day and a padded bra on the days I am not running or power walking. I try not to hate or to kill. I have gathered a lot of stones. I am ready for peace. I wonder if I am loving well.

Three times the Preacher answers his own question. In my favorite rendition he advises,

> Go, eat your food with gladness, and drink your wine with a joyful heart, for God has already approved what you do. Always be clothed in white, and always anoint your head with oil. (9:7–8)

That day on the island, after the blustery graveside service, I stuffed the Preacher's verses into my pocket, and we filed back down the backhoed road to our warehouse, where our fishing nets were kept. We had cleared the nets, set up sawhorses with plywood on top for tables, draped them with white sheets, and adorned them with sunny jars of wildflowers. We ate grilled salmon, pasta salad, salmonberry pies, and homemade bread. We drank coffee and traded stories about DeWitt, remembering his never-ending appetite for food and good friends. He lived a large, happy life.

Now at the end of this book, at the end of this essay, which I am writing last of all, I know for sure what this is. What I have been after from the start, though I did not know it from the start. Like the Preacher's book, ours too is a book of wonder and a book of wisdom. A collection of lives, words, and stories, all true, from women who have lived awhile and explored the deepest questions. Yes, these words are fallible. We are sinners still, all of us. But like the Preacher, we too have been guided on this wondrous looping path by the one Shepherd who goes before us all.

How does it end, then? In the Preacher's book, his questions and proverbs deliver us to an ending after all. After "all has been heard" (12:13), we arrive at the door of the house of the fragile man, the bent old woman whose teeth are few, whose sight is dimmed. Soon, he writes, their dust shall return "to the ground it came from" and their spirit shall return "to God who gave it" (12:7).

Some in these pages have already stepped onto the porch and through that door. In the several years of compiling this book, Win Couchman passed, joining Elisabeth Elliot and Madeleine L'Engle in their Father's glorious and happy house. We know this is our end too, which means it is also our beginning.

Here, then, standing before the wondrous eternal, the Preacher quits his proverbs. He lays down his literary pen, his enigmatic questions about the meaning of our lives, and speaks his answer now plain and straight:

> Now all has been heard;
>   here is the conclusion of the matter:
> Fear God and keep his commandments,
>   for this is the duty of all mankind.
> For God will bring every deed into judgment,
>   including every hidden thing,
>   whether it is good or evil.
>   (12:13–14)

Yes and amen. This is God-inspired truth. But I would like to end another way. As I close these pages of *The Wonder Years,* and as we approach the house with the door inched open, I can do no better than to quit my own words and end with God's, who knows what we need: "Even to your old age and gray hairs I am he, I am he who will sustain you. I have made you and I will carry you; I will sustain you and I will rescue you" (Isaiah 46:4).

Amen.

ACKNOWLEDGMENTS

The last anthology I edited (my third) was going to be my *last* anthology. Ever. Creating this kind of book is a bit like running a marathon through a swamp (I began this project five years ago). But I broke my own vow. I had to. As the decades piled up, I needed these women, their stories, their laughter, their wisdom. And I know a few million others who do as well.

I can't imagine a more fulfilling finish than what we now hold in our hands. The writer of Ecclesiastes complains at the end of his own book, "Of making many books there is no end, and much study wearies the body" (12:12). My flesh would be far wearier, this book would be far less, without the help of three women in particular: Jill Kandel, who has contributed two stunning essays as well as helped me edit the pieces I could not squeeze into my schedule. My faithful friend and reader Michelle Novak, also a contributor, offered constant support and prayer as well. Finally, I bow in gratitude to Dawn Anderson at Kregel, who went way beyond the call of duty to get this to press. Dawn, you were unwaveringly kind and generous in all your assistance. I owe you a spa day!

Thanks to my agent, Greg Johnson, who faithfully shepherded this passion project to the right people. And finally, huge thanks to Kregel for being the right people.

Finally, I thank every reader. If you haven't yet hit the Wonder Years, or if you are smartly in the midst of them, would you help us move the years of wonder beyond the covers of this book? Let's make this a movement of Holy Spirit–filled women rising up to bless the world with their hard-won wisdom, their contagious joy, their beautiful verve.